I believe
keep serving God
faithfully.

So, You Want to be a Man?

What Preachers Don't Preach and Fathers Don't Teach

Cornelius Lindsey

ISBN 978-0-9882187-8-9 (paperback)
ISBN 978-0-9882187-9-6 (digital edition)
For information regarding special discounts for
bulk purchases, please contact
info@corneliuslindsey.com.

www.corneliuslindsey.com

Printed in the U.S.A.

DEDICATION

I would like to dedicate this book to my son, Logan William Lindsey. You are one of the reasons I wake up in the morning. You motivate me to be a better man. You bring me joy and strength. I don't think you realize just how much I love you. I thank God daily that He is allowing me the opportunity to raise you. I'm so honored, son.

CONTENTS

Dear Brother,

I hope you're ready for an in-your-face type of encounter. The purpose of this book is to challenge you to become a man after God's heart. It is purposed to have you to confront the hurts of your past and deal with the pain caused by it. I don't know if your father abandoned you, but it's time to confront it. I know the feeling of being abandoned emotionally by your father. He is the very man who is meant to be instrumental in your life. You many not acknowledge the hurt it has caused, but it is time to confront it.

You may have picked up some bad habits along the way. Your sexual curiosity could entice you to experiment, which will only lead you down a deep, dark tunnel of despair. You may be in a place where you don't know where else to turn. You may be in search of answers. I know the pressure of engaging in pornography and allowing perversion to dwell in my heart. The pressures to watch pornography and have sex is all around us. It's seen and celebrated in movies, in music, on billboards, and literally everywhere you turn. Easy access to online porn adds more pressure to engage premarital sex, which is sex before marriage. The pornographic images displayed in our day is much more explicit, more pervasive, and a lot more violent than in the past. The pressure becomes a deadly combination when mixed with a surge teenage estrogen and testosterone. It's important to combat this pressure with graceful encouragement to resist. If proper boundaries, which encourage resistance, and important teachings of value and identity aren't prevalent in the home, you will start down a road that you won't like in the end. The curiosity, which is brought on by the intense pressure, pushes you to do things you never thought you would do. And unfortunately, you will think what you are doing is okay. I know what it's like to live a lie and commit acts that I'm ashamed to admit to anyone. It's time that you stopped trying to avoid these things. It's time to confront them head-on.

Maybe you have, or are, involved in a gang. Maybe you have sat around smoking blunts and marijuana, popping prescription pills in private, or engaged in sexual activity. Maybe you are looking for attention because you are not getting it at home. Or it could be that you desire to be like one of the cool kids. You might be one of the cool kids. It is important for you to know that drugs, alcohol, sex, popularity, or social media followers defines you. You may find comfort in those things, but they doesn't define you. They may soothe you, but they don't define you. Those things may help to take the edge off the pain and hurt of your reality, but it's time for you to deal with them. I know your pain is real because I have felt it. I've also had questions about the journey to manhood, and I know the joy I felt once I began to receive the answers. It's my honor to be able to share those answers with you.

I don't know if you hide behind a wall of insecurity. You may cover yourself with a blanket of pseudo-masculinity that is based on what you've learned rather than what is true. You may be a 'girl chaser' because you think that it's one way you can define your masculinity. Your attraction to other guys, children, or animals is but a secret right now, but, like so many men have found out, it will be made known. The little boy in you still wants to experiment and play. He has yet to mature. That little boy in you desires a man whom you respect and love to tell you that he loves you. He misses you. He believes in you. He stands beside you. He respects you.

It is my prayer that you are encouraged and built up from what you read. I hope you finish this book and you're able to say, "I know who I am!" That's true fulfillment! Knowing who you are will always be better than knowing what you should do. You are a human being, not a human doing. Focus more on finding your identity in Christ instead of concentrating on what you are supposed to do with your life. Most of the people around you are going to ask you the question: "What do you want to do in your life?" They are asking for you to identify your career. The question I am asking you is: "Who are you?" I want to know the man you are becoming, and I want you to identify him. You have purpose, and I believe in you! So when people ask you to identify what you want to do, tell them that you are discovering who you are. By discovering who you are first, your purpose will come to you.

Prepare for a rollercoaster ride and an epic encounter between you and God. I'm excited about your journey, and I pray that you come out purified, encouraged, enlightened, courageous, and empowered to continue. I stand with you. Know that you can do this! You can be a man after God's heart.

God bless.

Respectfully,

Cornelius Lindsey

THE END

I read Proverbs 5 daily. It's an encouraging wise tale of a son not listening to his father. He's encouraged to avoid the adulteress, but he refuses. After having all he had snatched from him, he realized his mistakes. Unfortunately, it was too late. Temptation led him away into sin, and sin led him to destruction. Proverbs 5 is a warning to avoid temptation so you won't have to suffer the consequences of sin. While it won't be your end, it will definitely feel like it. This chapter is an expounding on Proverbs 5. Many of my mistakes can be found in what you are about to read. This is a mixture of my failures and some of the failures of other men I've met. Although the Lord has redeemed and restored both myself and those affected by my mistakes, I want to illuminate the reality of the very real ramifications of carnal decisions. It's my desire that you are encouraged to resist temptation. Be encouraged.

I sit in silence wondering what has led me to this place of shame and agony. I was once at the height of my success. I worked hard to gain the trust of my peers and the community. I spent many days consoling others, giving to others, and forgiving others under the harshest circumstances. But now I sit all alone on the edge of my bed in my room with a pistol by my side. My wife has divorced me. My wealth is all gone. My children have gone astray, and my reputation has gone to ruin. I am no longer the man of integrity I once was in my community. I am now the subject of many cruel and evil jeers that are heard each time I step out of my house. I cannot stop crying. I cannot seem to wipe the sinful stain from what was once a sinless record. All I worked for has gone to ruin, and I cannot wash the smell of the adulteress from my body.

I was told countless times not to flirt with her. I was told not to enter her house or stroll with her around time, but I did not listen. I knew the warning of destruction and ruin that was to follow my relationship with her, but I did not heed it. I guess I was willing to risk the end at the beginning because I did not know the pain, agony, shame, and soon-coming death at the end. I failed to keep my eyes on eternity. Instead, I was focused on the present. I was focused on getting my "fix." I have been clean for years. I have abstained for years. I have put off the temptress for years. I have been able to successfully escape the punishment that followed my sinful ways, but I have been found out. I have been caught in the temptresses trap. Now, I am all-alone. The pain is too much to bear. The agony is too much to take on.

I sat all last night asking myself why I turned away from what I knew to be true. I could not understand why I did not incline my ear to hear the truth. I was trying to reason with why I was willing to face the consequence of my action without fully understanding the shame of it all. Yet, I could not find a logical answer. I wish I could say that I did not know, but that would be a lie! I wish I could say that I was never told, but that would be a lie! I wish I could have said that the sin was more enticing than the truth, but that was a lie!

Now, I sit here with my pistol by my side reliving my horrible mistakes over the last couple of days. I knew I should not have gone to that liquor store. I rationalized with myself that I deserved to go. I deserved to go get a bottle of liquor to ease my stress and calm my nerves. I was looking for my answer at the end of the bottle instead of going to prayer like I normally did on Saturday night. I went to my man cave, which was set-aside for me to go and meet God daily, and it was there that I continued to drink until the bottle was empty. Then in my inebriation, my ability to rationalize slowly went away. I was no longer in my right mind. I sat there with the phone in my hand, and I sent a text message to someone who I knew was only out for trouble. I had spurned the adulteress's advances before, but my inability to rationalize at this point allowed me to go forward with what my wicked heart desired.

There I was sitting in my chair with my Bible opened, but I did not turn to read it. I did not turn to heed the words of truth that comprise it. I was still focused on what I was about to get into that night. Then, the doorbell rings. I go to answer it without hesitation. I opened the door wide to allow for the adulteress to come in to the very place I would sit and commune with my Father. Once inside, the adulteress grabbed me by my hips and pressed closely against my body. We embraced and kissed like we had missed each other for years. This exchange led to a night of sinful, passionate sex that would serve to my ruin.

As I lie there asleep, I hear my phone ringing. I jump up to answer it, but I missed the call. Then, I hear a rattle at that door. I run to try to catch the person entering before she or he comes in to discover me in my sin, but I was too late. The door swings open, and there stands my wife. She has a look of disgust on her face, and she realizes the situation she has found me is not a good one.

Unable to keep my strength, I fall down to my knees in my nakedness. The adulteress jumps from my bed with a big smile. My wife begins to sob and cry uncontrollably, and I am too weak to go over to console her. With the last amount of strength I have, I look at her to and said, "Please let me explain." Without hesitation, she rushes out the door.

There I was on my knees in the very spot I once went to the Lord in prayer. This time was different. This time I was exposed and naked. I was barren and without life. I was caught up in the adulteress's trap after years and years of denying the adulteress's advances. I began to weep loudly because the pain and agony of the situation was far too much to bear. I could not understand what led to me that place. I tried to reason with myself to think how my wife had a part to play in this mess, but it did not work. I knew I was at the center of the problem. My sin was found out, and I was finally exposed before those who loved me.

Hours later, I began to get calls from people who once respected me. They wanted to know if what they heard was true. I could not lie to them. I had to tell them the truth. Then, I received a call from the elders of the church asking me to come in for an emergency meeting. There I sat in front of a group of men who once respected me highly. This meeting was not so I could hear the plight of the church or the needs of the people. Instead, this meeting was for me to tell them how I was caught in the adultery. I was there to tell them how my lies and deceit found me out. I tried to reason with them that it was because I felt alone and abandoned. I tried to tell them that I was in need of some gratification and satisfaction, but they did not buy my lies for one second. One of the elders stood to her feet and he told me I had to step down as pastor. Those were the words I did not want to hear, but I knew they were righteous words.

As I drove home, I could not stop crying. I walked into my house to find a letter and divorce papers. The letter read:

I am not sure how I can say this, but I must say it. I have been faithful to you in all of our years of marriage. I was there for you when everyone else turned their back on you. I was there for you when you had absolutely nothing. I was there for you when no one knew your name. I was there for you when everyone else said I should leave. I defended your name when other people would defile you in my presence. I was there, and this is the way you treat me? I have left the divorce papers near this letter. I have taken the children, and we will be at my parent's home. I am beyond hurt, and I am so ashamed. I will send someone else over to retrieve the rest of our things from the house. I realize our children love you, and I want to give you every opportunity to spend as much time with them as possible. They do not deserve to be used as pawns in this crazy game. Thank you for breaking my heart and ruining my life.

Signed,

Your Ex-Wife

After reading the letter, I cried and wailed loudly. I screamed from the top of my lungs, "How have I hated instruction!" I could not understand how I refused to listen to what was true and righteous.

It does not matter now because my life has been ruined. My sin has stolen my honor and majesty, the years of my life, all that I have labored and worked hard to gain, my influence, my wealth, and my family. Honestly, sin did not take it from me. I freely gave it up when I entered in to sin's house and agreed to its' advances. Now my family is ruined. My influence is gone. My wealth is swallowed up. I have nothing to my name. I am sick as I have ever been in my entire life, and I am so ashamed!

Now, I sit here on the edge of my bed with my pistol beside me. I no longer have a reason to live. I am the man! I refused to follow the commands of God. I refused to receive His love and guidance. I am a man most miserable, and I've been humbled. Now, I realize that I'm not a man at all. I am but a male posing as a man. I am left with one great desire. I desire to be a man, God's man.

THE BOY

As a pastor, I deal with parents who desire for their son(s) to change. They want their son(s) to be transformed into what they refer to as "good young men." I also encounter parents who will tell me that their son(s) is a "good boy" because he has never gone to jail. Parents, I hate to burst your bubble, but my mom also considered me a "good boy." I sat down with my mom one Saturday evening, and I told her stories about all the crazy things I had done. I told her about all the times I should have been arrested for my actions. She did not have a clue about any of it. I was not the guy on the corner selling drugs in plain sight. Oh, no, I was much worse. I was the charming boy who did all my dirt in private. I was the boy who planned all my evil deeds while everyone else was asleep. Then, I would convince others to do the deeds for me. I was like what most men are today—cowards. Those parents, like my mom, thought I was good because I did not go to jail. That is far from the truth. I was just favored enough that I did not get caught, or I was pardoned for my actions. I always ask those parents about their son(s) actions. By learning about the son(s) actions I am able to understand his heart. If his heart is resting peacefully in the hands of God, then I fully expect to hear that he gives constant attention to prayer, to fasting, to studying the

Scriptures, etc. He spends his time practicing and perfecting spiritual disciplines. If his heart is far from God, I fully expect to hear that he is out partying, playing video games, focused on sports, etc. Please do not get me wrong. I am not saying that sports or video games are wrong, but I am saying they are wrong when they are given precedence over his time of prayer, studying of Scripture, fasting, etc. If God holds his heart, he will be sensitive to what video games he plays. In fact, he probably will not have that desire to play them anyway. He will desire to spend more of his time growing his relationship with God.

Nonetheless, it never fails that a parent will want me to talk to his/her son. In the beginning of my ministry, I would definitely comply. I would go and sit and talk with these young men, but it would seem like they would not listen or understand what I was saying. I felt like I was going in circles with them. It felt like I was hitting a brick wall. Years later, I was in prayer, and the Lord began to deal with me about the entire process. I want to share it with you right now in the form of a situation. After you read the situation, I will explain it to you.

There was a young, single mother who was tasked with raising 4 children on her own. She had one son and three daughters. She spent most of their childhood working 2, and sometimes 3, jobs at a time just to make ends meet. The children spent most of their time at random babysitters' houses. The mother did not have much time to devote to the children because she was trying her best to just keep a roof over their head and food in their belly. The three girls would find time to play with each other, but the boy would venture off into his room to play video games, watch television, and listen to music. Because the mother felt sorry that she could not be very active in his life, she would buy him all the video games he wanted, whether they were x-rated or not. She just bought them. She would get him certain cds that were filled with violence and hate. She allowed him to have a television in his room where he could watch any television he wanted, no matter how graphic the show. As years went by, this young mother began having constant problems with her son. He was constantly being suspended from school from violence, he had a very violent temper, he secretly started smoking, he was getting pornography from his friends at school, and he did not respect his mother at all. He even went as far as telling his mother and sisters that he would kill them all if they did not leave him alone.

One day, the mother had enough, so she went to her pastor's office to speak with him about her son. She told him everything her son was doing with tears rolling down her face. She was trying to figure out what was going wrong. She wanted to have some answers on where she went wrong with her son. She felt as if she gave him everything he wanted. She would discipline him when he was young. He always had food to eat and a place to lay his head. He never had to work for anything. She felt like he should have come out as a great child, but he was far from it. She has taken him to a certified counselor and a psychiatrist, but none of them worked for him. She wanted her pastor to cast a demon out of him because she felt like that was the exact problem.

The pastor sat back in his chair, and told the mother that he would talk to him. The mother convinced her son to go see the pastor. After church that Sunday, the boy walked into the pastor's office. They sat there and talked for hours. Then, the boy finally broke down and began to weep. The pastor embraced the young man, and told him to meet him at his home that following Tuesday to discuss more of his situation. The boy did as the pastor said, and they continued to meet for months. The boy began to see the pastor as a father in his life, and he felt as if he was making some real changes. Then, there came that winter night when the pastor's family was all gone. The pastor called the boy over to his home to keep him company. The boy went over and lay with his pastor in the bed like he always did. As the boy was drifting off to sleep, he felt a masculine hand rub up his inner thigh. The boy quickly jumped out of the bed, looked at the pastor, and was conflicted on what he should do. He did not want to hurt the only man who seemed to show him some attention, but he did not want to be exposed to that kind of relationship. Not wanting to hurt the pastor, the boy got back in the bed, and that night became one of he worst experiences of his life. The boy was exposed and opened to an entire world he had never considered before. Now, the conflict within the boy was greater than anything he had ever imagined.

Now, I am going to stop right here so I can explain to you the situation that you have just read.

First, this mother is to be applauded for her hard work in doing what she thought was right in raising her children. She stepped up to the plate, and did not pass the responsibility off to anyone. That is first and foremost.

I in no way want to seem like I am blaming or exposing the mother, as if she is insignificant. However, the young man lacked a very vital ingredient in his life; he lacked a father. He lacked the guidance necessary for him to maturate successfully from a boy to a man. The boy was clueless, just like many other boys are today. The father was not there to actively teach him Scripture and show him the example he is called to follow. This was missing in this boy's life, and sadly, it is missing in many men's lives. Truthfully, this is where the elders and the pastor should come to the rescue. The care for widows is a covenant community responsibility that is shown in Acts 6:1. The verse reads, "Now at this time while the disciples were increasing in number, a complaint arose on the part of the Hellenistic Jews against the native Hebrews, because their widows were being overlooked in the daily serving of food." Based on this verse, caring for the widows was something that was seen as a responsibility in the early church. It is not seen in that light today. James 1:27 reads, "This is pure and undefiled religion in the sight of our God and Father, to visit orphans and widows in their distress, and to keep oneself unstained by the world." This is a vital truth; yet, many have abandoned the responsibility of caring for the orphans and the widows. Between 1941 and 1945, many men were leaving their families to go fight in World War II. This was an admirable thing, but it left the mother home alone to raise the children, teach the children, feed the children, care for the children, etc. This also led to the children adopting their own way of living what they thought was acceptable based on sociological standards. Many of those children had to grow up without their father being home, and many had to deal with the emotional and physiological issues that their father brought home because of the war. The family was essentially broken. The mother was tasked with multiple responsibilities, the father was away at war, and the children did what was right in their own mind. It was a giant free-for-all.

Now, this boy had something the children in the 30's did not have. He had cable television in his room, video games, an iPhone, and all the name-brand clothing he wanted. As you read, his mother bought him all of these things because she felt sorry for him. She felt bad that his father was not in his life, she was not able to devote more of her time to him, and she wanted him to have what he wanted. She thought it was a good thing. However, remember when I said that he lacked that influential guidance in his life? Well, in some ways he did have it. It just was not his father. Instead of being taught by his father, he was taught by television shows, music, video games, etc. He would listen to certain songs throughout the night after school that would alter his way of thinking. For hours, he would listen to songs about violence, hatred, sex, disrespect, and rebellion. He would then watch television shows that should not even be watched by adults because of the perverted nature of the show. He would watch movies late at night that would awaken lust inside of him and breed perversion. This lustful thinking that was growing in his heart from all the music and television led him to begin texting little girls. This led to sexting, a form of texting where someone sends sexually-explicit messages or pictures. He did this for years locked away in his room while his mother was at work and his sisters were enjoying one another's company. He learned everything he knows about sex from pornographic movies he got from his friends at school. He watched for hours as the men dehumanize women in the films, so he took it as a way of life. He saw the men dehumanize women, he heard the singers and rappers dehumanize women, so he also dehumanized women. His actions began to show what was in his heart.

As you also read, the mother was quick to give him what he wanted, but she failed to give him what he needed. Again, this is in no way a direct insult towards the mother. My goal is to show the importance of having guidance in the boy's life. See, the mother constantly gave the boy clothes, a phone, etc. because he wanted it. However, God never gives a command for parents to give their child what they want. Rather, he instructs for parents to give their child what they need. A child may not want the rod of correction, but that does not mean you should spare it. A child may not want to sit and be taught Scripture, but it is for his or her own welfare. See, parents cannot be so concerned about getting a child what he or she wants without first ensuring that they have what they need. God is a righteous and good Father who gives His children all we need. We have food even if it is not the food we want. We have shelter even if it is not the shelter we want. The need has been fulfilled. Earthly parents must think the same way.

Also, the mother did not make her son work for anything. She just gave it to him. This is very dangerous. A boy must learn how to work, and how to work hard. He must learn how to accumulate wealth little by little so he appreciates it later. I witnessed a father instruct his son in this way. While his son was out mowing the grass, he noticed that the top of the fence posts had fallen off and into the grass. Well, the top of the fence posts were visible, but his son still ran them over with the lawnmower. After his son finished cutting the grass, he walked up to his son and asked him for $25.00 out of his allowance. The son was shocked; however, the dad was proving a point. His son ruined 5 tops that sit atop the fence when he ran over them. The father was charging his son $5.00 for each one because he failed to pay attention to what he was doing. Some may say that the father could have been a little more lenient; however, this is a lesson the son will always remember. Now, he knows the importance of paying attention to what he is doing, and he realizes the importance of how he can lose his wealth if he is not careful. The boy in the example could have used a lesson like this, and I think it would have definitely helped. It definitely helped me.

When I was a boy, my mom and dad would make me wake up early every Saturday morning to mow the lawn. I *hated* mowing the lawn, and I hated that I would have to miss Bugs Bunny. However, it was a family affair. My mom would be on the riding-mower, my dad would have the weed-eater, I would have the push-mower, and my sister would have the rake. We would be outside from sun-up until sun-down. Yes, we had a lot of yard to cut. It was exhausting work. At the end of the day, my parents would reward my sister and I with pizza or Chinese food, and we would get an allowance. The allowance meant something because I worked so hard for it. I sweated out of my clothes for it. Therefore, I would think twice before wasting it. As I got older, that work ethic stuck with me. When I was 15, I got a job working in a concession stand. It was food and customer service, so it was doubly hard for me. But, I worked hard every opportunity I got. I worked hard, and I saved enough money to buy my first car with cash. The car was a grey 1994 Mazda Protégé. That was my baby, and I took care of it because I knew how hard it was to work for it. I worked at that job for years. Sometimes, I would have to work long hours. I would work 23 hours at times, but that is what I had to do in order to save my money. When I got ready to go off to college, my parents did not have to pay a dime. I paid for my college applications. When I was accepted, I paid for the trip down there. I paid for all of my books. I paid for everything I needed in my dormroom. It was an amazing feeling to know that I worked hard, and I could enjoy the fruit of my labor. My parents instilled that hard work ethic in me early in life.

There was one fall where I thought my hard work was coming to an end because it was starting to come to an end. My mom had told my sister and me that we would not have to cut the grass anymore that year because the cold weather was causing it not to grow. I was relieved. However, I came home from school one day to find 3 calves in a newly built cow pen. I was trying to figure out what in the world we were going to do with them. My mom and dad introduced me to a big bottle and a powdered formula. I would hear the calves mooing loudly outside; then, my mom would come in my room and tell me to go and feed the calves. It would be 4:30am, but I had to get up and feed the calves. I would have to sit there as they drank milk out of the bottles. I had to do this all winter. It was tough, but it taught me discipline. When the next summer came around, our freezer was full of meat. It was an awesome feeling to know my diligence and work ethic helped to provide for my family. Yes, all I did was feed the calves, but if I didn't feed them, they would die.

If your mother or father have not instilled within you work ethic, then you may not yet understand the value of what is given to you. Much like the boy, you will become spoiled rotten. And although you may enjoy the video games, shoes, and the car that you're given, if you haven't earned anything, then you'll grow into a man who expects things to be handed to him. Sir, you do not want this. This will strip you of your own masculinity. A man lives unfulfilled without meaningful work in his life. Every boy needs work—hard work. You need to learn the art of work, discipline, integrity, character, etc. You must experience the feeling of working hard for something and being able to enjoy the fruits of it. The only time work becomes dangerous is when it takes priority over God. Don't depend on your mother to give you what you want, the way that this boy did. Instead you must work for what you want. Take it upon yourself to learn the purpose of money; otherwise you will abuse it. Anything you do not know the purpose of, you are bound to pervert and abuse. There is no way around it.

Before addressing the issue with between the boy and the pastor, I want to bring one more key thing to your attention. Did you notice that the mother did all of those things for her son, took him to counseling, and took him to get psychoanalysis;

yet, he still did not change? I want you to pay attention to this. The mother desires for her son to have biblical standards of masculinity, but the boy has been trained in carnality. *What does that mean, Cornelius?* I am glad you asked. Much like this boy who has been guided and trained by the songs he listened to, the movies he watched, and the friends he had, you may have been trained in carnality, or the ways of the flesh, too. Ways of the flesh are the opposite of the ways of God. See, I am sure the mom was taking the boy to church when she was able to go. I am sure she was giving him a couple of Scriptures she heard the pastor say on a couple of occasions; however, none of those things worked. Is this the case in your home as well? You mother's faith may not be motivating you to change. What every boy needs, and what you need is a purposed-filled guidance of manhood. You need a man who was committed to teaching and leading you into manhood. The boy did not have it; however, the mother expected the boy to understand true, biblical masculinity even though he was never trained in that way. Instead, he was trained in carnality. See, the boy spent 18 years of his life being trained and led by the world, or carnality. As you read, he was acting out, and his mother could no longer control him. She wanted to know how to help him. Well, his actions began to reflect his nature. The boy meditated and was trained in the ungodliness, and his nature reflected it. His heart was filled with perversion, sex, violence, hatred, envy, jealousy, etc. because that is what he was taught from the music and the television shows. He gave his attention to it, and whatever you meditate on the most is what you will worship. First, all of the ungodliness got into his heart. Then, his actions began to show what was already inside of him. Proverbs 4:23 reads, "Watch over your heart with all diligence, for from it flow the springs of life." Do you realize the significance of the heart, and why it was important for his mother to help him guard it? Do you understand your own responsibility in guarding your heart? Your mother cannot push you forever—you must make the decision to grow. Despite what other boys in school do, I assure you that you will not miss out if you're given everything that you want. You will be fine. You do not need the access to dirty channels or be tempted to listen to music that will pollute your heart. You may not understand the ramifications of your actions now, but you will. Unwanted pregnancies, STD's, spiritual soul-ties, addiction, depression, regret, shame, embarrassment and loss are all very real consequences for your unguarded heart. Everyday men who are married with families have to sift through the pain and regret of the decisions made in their youth. As a boy, you may already very adventurous and curious. When you mix curiosity with ungodliness, you are ready for a dangerous outcome. Allowing yourself the opportunity to be alone with the world without fully understanding the dangers of it is like giving a child a loaded gun and expecting him not to harm himself. As you're nearing manhood, you must decipher what is dangerous and head in the opposite direction. Your mother or father will not take the fall for your decisions forever.

Lastly, we must address the issue that is plaguing many relationships and churches today. That is the predator who lives to lure the bait in only to attack on the prey when it is at its weakest. I know so many mothers, especially single mothers, who had no where else to turn but to the Boys Scouts leader, the pastor, the counselor, the teacher, etc. for help with their son(s). She took her son there for help, but all he got was hurt. Many times, the boy comes out of a situation like this much worse than how we went in. The predator feeds off of the boy's innocence, immaturity, and childlikeness. He finds the preys weakest point; then, he bites until there is no life left in him. The prey is never free until he breaks from the grip of the predator.

One Sunday after church a pastor confronted me. I admit my wrong in the situation. He looked me in the eyes, and he scolded me until I broke. I had endured many hurtful and insulting verbal lashings, but I could not stand any more of it. I looked the pastor in the eyes and said, "Why do you treat me this way? I feel like I am your dog!" He looked at me, and said, "Yeah, you are right. You are my dog." I will never forget those words. Tears began to roll down my eyes as I stood there in front of him. I totally blanked out at that moment as he continued to talk. Then, he moved closer to me, and he embraced me with a hug. But, I did not bring my arms up to touch him. I put on my sunglasses, and I walked to my car with my wife. At that moment, I realized I was in the hands of an abusive relationship. However, I was determined to be obedient to God at all costs. I finally escaped that grip; however, some are not so bold to do it.

This boy had a major conflict growing inside of him after he felt the masculine caress of the pastor's hands around his inner thigh. Because of the hunger for guidance and masculine attention, the boy did not want to lose what he saw as a gift. This is the same feeling many women have who are in abusive relationships. The boy did not want to hurt the pastor, so he chose to sleep with him instead. Now, the boy has to deal with other issues compiled onto the issues he brought into the relationship.

Does it tug at your heart like it does mine to know there are countless boys in the world today who have to endure this same situation? There are stadiums filled with men, jails filled with men, golf courses filled with men, boardrooms filled with men, etc.; however, why are they not at home caring, leading, and guiding their son(s)? I bet you want to know the answer to the question I am about to pose to you right now. Here it is: Where are the men? Well, go to the next chapter and find out.

SILENT AND ABSENT FATHER

I don't think there is a greater relationship for a son to have except that with his father. The confirming words of a man's father gives him reassurance that he is progressing effectively. The father has a chance to mold the boy into the man by teaching and instilling in him the characteristics that are oftentimes lost in our modern society. The father is given a great responsibility to not only teach the living word of God but to be a living example of it. The son is given an opportunity to see the words of Scripture brought to life in the example set by his father. It's an honor for the son to watch his father love his mother, provide spiritually and physically for his family, teach with passion and fervor, and assist, when needed, for the greater good of his community with the fatherless and widows.

I, like so many, was not given a perfect example. Honestly, I don't believe any son has been given a perfect example. Nonetheless, I honor my father. Unlike a lot of fathers, my father chose to stay in my life. He was present, yet he was silent.

I oftentimes hear young men talk about the pain of not having their father in the home. They talk about having to learn how to become a man by watching those they admire from afar. Some learn to take certain traits from the men they see. From there, they try to assemble the perfect picture or idea of what they think a man is. Unfortunately, many of those qualities they see in other men aren't qualities that are found in God. My heart breaks for those men whose earthly father is absent, and it is torn for those men whose father is present yet silent.

For years, I would sit in the same house with my father; yet, he would never teach me. My older sister was his favorite, and he didn't try to hide it. I felt rejected by him as if I didn't measure up in many ways. I was never into sports, but I would try to be because I knew my dad loved them. He worked long hours, so I barely saw him during the week. When he was home, he would eat, drink his beer, and go to bed. There were not many words said between the two of us. I always knew when he was home because the remote control would go into his hands. He would surf the channels until he found a game on television, whether it was basketball or football. If none of those games were on, we would watch ESPN. I felt like I knew a way to get my father to recognize me, so I chose to play minor league sports. I started off with baseball. I went to the practices, but, honestly, they didn't do much help. The coach put me in the outfield for the first game. There I was, standing out in the hot sun waiting for someone to send a ball my way. Suddenly, one of the big guys went up to the plate. He hit the ball as hard as he could. At that moment, I knew it was my chance to shine. I screamed out to everyone to get back because that ball was mine. After what felt like eternity for the ball to get to me, I noticed it was going much faster than I anticipated. I reached my glove up to catch the ball, but it missed it completely. Instead, the ball hit me right on the top of the head. There I was lying flat on the ground after being hit with the ball on the top of the head. The coach came out, checked on me, and I finally woke up. While waking up, all I could hear was my mother's voice screaming at me to wake up. He voice would become a staple for all of my competitive events, whether sports or academic. I opened my eyes to see that my father wasn't there. That was my first game, and it was also my last. I never played baseball after that.

Months later, I noticed how much my father loved basketball. His face lit up when the games were on. He knew the names of the players. He knew their stats and everything. I was so jealous because I wanted him to want to know me that way, so I decided I was going to play basketball. I went to the first practice where we had to scrimmage against one another. On one side were the skins and the shirts were on the other. Unfortunately, I got chosen for the skins, and my chest wasn't anything that needed to be shown to anyone. I was short and chubby, so you know I was picked on. It felt like I was doing the Harlem shake each time I ran. It was horrendous, and decided I wasn't going to play basketball anymore. My dad never made it to that practice.

Finally, I was entering the seventh grade, and I had to make a decision to either play football or join the band. Well, I wasn't one for being in the band, so I decided I'd give football a shot. I ended up playing for 2 years, and I would like to think that I got better over time. I never understood the plays. I played left guard and center on offense, and I played nose guard on defense. I don't think I played those things because I was that good. I played them because I was that big. Remember, I was a chubby kid. For two years, I would see my mom in the stands cheering me on. There was one game where my father decided to show up. I'll never forget it. We were down a touchdown against one of our rivals, Philadelphia. I glanced towards the bleachers, and I saw my mother and sister sitting there. Then, I saw my father walked in through the entrance. We were at the bottom of the third quarter, and I was pumped up. I was about to show my father what kind of son he had. That was my proving time. As the quarterback made the play, I shot the ball up to his hands. He went back to throw the ball, and, out of nowhere, it started to rain. Everyone started to scramble. People were running to their cars, but the game was still going on. Then, the whistle sounds, and the game was put on hold. The team was escorted to the locker room until the rain slowed up. About fifteen minutes later, we went back out there, and we were all drenched from the rain. I looked out towards the bleachers and my mom and sister were standing under the bleachers. My dad was nowhere in sight. We ended up losing that game. I went home, and my dad was there. He had already started drinking. I told myself that he came to see me, but he left because it was raining. My mother thought it was important enough to stay, but he didn't. That was a tough pill to swallow.

Once I entered high school, I stopped trying to impress my father. I thought it was a senseless pursuit. Instead, I began to try to find myself. I was born and partly raised in a rural town in Mississippi; however, I started high school in the congested, city life of Georgia. It was already a huge transition for me to go from middle school to high school. I had added stress because I was beginning a new life in a new world around new people, and I desperately wanted everything to go back to normal. During my ninth grade school year, I was bullied. The kids were much bigger than me. The guys were taller, and I was still short and chubby. I was called all kinds of names. They would comment about my clothes, and they would oftentimes throw things at me. I didn't have any friends, so I would eat alone. I would buy more than one lunch because I was always so hungry. So, yes, I was the chubby kid who would sit in the back of the cafeteria with more than one lunch. There was one incident where I was sitting in the cafeteria eating my lunches when a twelfth grader came up from behind me. He snatched my cookies from in front of me. I stood up to get them back, and he proceeded to run around the cafeteria urging me to chase him. At that moment, everyone began to laugh at me. It was the worst feeling in the world simply because I felt like everyone had always been laughing at me since I was a child. I failed at baseball. Most folks laughed at me when that ball hit me in the top of the head. I failed at basketball. When I took off my shirt, the laughs started, and they really didn't stop. I couldn't find anything that I could say I was successful at doing. I felt like I was a failure at being a son. All that failure was too much for me to handle. I remember going home, locking my bedroom door, and hoping that I died. I was tired of feeling like a failure. I decided to focus on academics. I began to excel. Then, I chose to focus on extracurricular clubs and organizations. I became the president of my class, and I served as a high-ranking officer in many clubs like the Future Farmers of America, Future Business

Leaders of America, Key Club, and the list goes on. I was captain of the Mock Trial, debate, and Model United Nations team. I began to compete in many competitions, from impromptu speaking to gardening. In every awards ceremony I was involved in, my father didn't show up. I would receive many awards for academic and extracurricular success, but my father was never there to see it.

My relationship with him continued to decline, and my feeling of being a failure began to subside. However, I became more and more prideful. I was finally finding myself, and I felt as if I did it all on my own. I felt as if I didn't need God, my father, or anyone else. I was all into myself, and the pedestal I built for myself was higher than my ego.

I would love to know what my life would've been like to have a father who was able to lead and guide me in all truth. Unfortunately, that wasn't a hand I was dealt. I had to make due with what was given to me. Ultimately, God began to humble me. During that period of my life, I began to see my father in a new light. He was no longer the man I despised for his silence. I began to feel sorry for him. I wanted him to experience the same love from God that I was experiencing. I realized that he wouldn't go to God on his own, so I had to be the example of love for him. Ultimately, I realized this great truth. Even though my father was silent, that didn't mean I had to be. The same is true for you. Just because your father is absent, that doesn't mean you have to be. Just because your father is an alcoholic, adulterer, liar, murderer, drug addict, or thief, it doesn't mean that you have to be. I want to encourage you to stop using the absence or silence of your father as an excuse for your inability to follow Christ fully. Begin to focus in on Christ, and pursue Him. Instead of trying to shape yourself after another man, allow the Spirit of God to begin to do such a work in you that you don't even recognize you.

Sir, your father could be absent or silent, but that doesn't mean God is. Pursue Him with passion!

TO BE THE STUDENT

Knowing is one thing; becoming is another.

I've been a student for many years. This is not a great thing because anyone can essentially be student. It doesn't take much. The student searches diligently for knowledge from the teacher. The student functions logically, rationally. As he continues to gather more and more knowledge, he becomes more and more knowledgeable. Soon enough, he will become the teacher, but he never ceases being a student. One day he'll realize that all he ever was taught and all he ever learned was borrowed. Even his own generalizations are based on material passed down from generation to generation.

The student is pseudo-learner; he is a carbon-copy existence. The student studies for hours learning about God; however, he has yet to know God himself. He learns about peace, but he has yet to truly experience peace. He understands the concept of joy; yet, he has never experienced it on his own. He may be knowledgeable about writing music; however, he has never experienced the beauty of soothing musical lyrics. He is very knowledgeable of many things; yet, he knows absolutely nothing. The light that should shine out of him is dark like it was from his beginning. He knows much, but he knows nothing.

He can sit and discuss theory, but he has yet to grasp the truth. That's because he has searched for truth in words. He has journeyed to find truth lurking in the text of the Bible. He has yet to understand that truth lives far beyond the Scriptures. It exists far above the printed words. However, he must know that the beginning of all truth begins at the Scriptures. They cannot be ignored or looked over.

The student is the foremost character in any classroom who is filled with great knowledge but little-to-no understanding of what he studies. The disciple, however, is a different breed of man. He was once the student, but he has matured.

The disciple takes all that he has learned, and he seeks to become it rather than just know it. He doesn't just learn about Christ. He seeks to become Christ. He seeks to live out his life just like Christ lived out His. He doesn't just learn about love. He seeks to become love. He doesn't just care about learning truth. He scours the Scriptures not to just be knowledgeable of truth, rather, he searches Scripture with hopes that he may become truth. He endeavors to live a life that exemplifies truth. The student reads and studies the map. The map is important to him because it shows him the direction if he ever chose to journey. However, once he matures to be the disciple, he finds the map to be a great treasure. The disciple uses the map in the journey. He takes slow, prudent steps so that he will not steer off the path the map is taking him.

The student is not in danger. He doesn't take any risk. He merely learns about love, but he never takes the risk to become love to the unlovely. He learns about sacrifice, but he never becomes sacrificial. He learns about service, but he doesn't serve. He takes no risk beyond the words. In fact, it's like the words have encaged him, and that is where he chooses to stay.

On the other hand, the disciple takes uncalculated risks. He dives into the deep abyss having nothing more than all he was once taught as a student. Some disciples don't even have the knowledge. They weren't given the privilege of being as educated as the student. However, it doesn't bother the disciple. The disciple enjoys going into the uncharted sea. He finds it more important to journey rather than just read. The books bore him. They are used to supplement his time rather than consume it.

Consider colleges and universities today. They are filled with great hoarders, men and women who gather knowledge the same way the greedy man gathers wealth. To the student, knowledge is his wealth. He aspires for more knowledge until he sees that he cannot be taught anymore, so he chooses to unload all that his mind carries to an awaiting hoarder. The student is greedy; he is knowledge-driven.

The disciple is a totally different phenomenon. He does not try to hoard. He desires to explore and journey. He wants to experience. He wants to risk it all. In fact, he has to risk it all. He cannot take anything with him on his journey. He understands that even all he has been taught it useless in certain environments. The words he heard and read were without meaning and carried no life because they were heard while he sat comfortably in safety. He understands that it is one thing teach a class on fishing; it is another to actually go out and fish.

The student wants to know about God. His relationship with God is a 'head relationship.' He connects with God mentally, and that is all. His growth is stunted. He only knows from borrowed experience. He reads the words of Paul, yet he doesn't anguish. Why? It is because the words mean nothing to him! They are mere words written in an insignificant book. Because of the insignificance, the student finds comfort in challenging what he has studied. He stands before men and teaches heresy because he has adopted his own revelation of what he was learning. He is only a student, but that has yet to sink into his head. For some reason, he stops his journey there. He fails to realize he must mature far beyond the pages of the open book. He must explore and become. But, the student chooses not to explore. He finds no reason to explore. His is connected with God with his head. He grows in knowledge, and that is all.

The disciple's relationship with the Savior is one of the heart. It is a love relationship that the world cannot fathom. They find it odd how the disciple can love beyond the words of Scripture. The world finds it strange that the disciple can see beyond the literary works of aged students to journey into unknown territory reserved only for those who choose to journey. The disciple's love causes him to jump from his desk and rush out of the room even if it means leaving his map behind.

Saul, later known as Paul, was a man who vehemently hated and murdered many Christians during his lifetime. He despised Christianity because he was raised in a religious environment that taught him to strictly follow rules—not the living God, Jesus Christ. On his way traveling to a town called Damascus, Saul had a miraculous encounter with God that he could not deny. He was converted immediately. From then on, Saul was known as Paul. Look at the love demonstrated by Paul on the road to Damascus. After his experience, Paul was connected to the Savior with his heart and not his head. He left behind all that he knew to fearlessly dive into the unknown territory of serving the Savior he once persecuted others for loving. That is great love!

Like Paul, we must endeavor to be great disciples and not students. A disciple understands that he must merge with the Master. He literally eliminates all distances and bridges between himself and the Master. This is not so that he cannot get to Him. He destroys the distances and bridges after he has crossed them and traveled them so that he can have no option of returning to what he once knew. The disciple effaces himself and completely surrenders. He counts all that he had as nothing alone with himself. In his sincere humility, his heart opens so the Master may take refuge. In his humility, his ego vanishes, and the Master journeys deeply into his being. The disciple finds himself vulnerable and unguarded. He is receptive to the words of the Master. He studies the Bible; however, he doesn't study it like the student. In fact, he cannot. Every word of Scripture is so precious to the disciple because he lives it rather than just memorizing it. He drops to his knees at even the most insignificant verse because it pierces him in the heart. The disciple drops all he has in his hand. He takes everything away from his eye. He doesn't allow his tongue to taste what it once loved. His footsteps are sensitive, and his words are guided. His defense against God is weak. In fact, it is demolished; nonexistent. This allows God to work in and through him.

While the student studies exactly what he is told, the disciple is living it out. The disciple is so committed through love to God that he has made a conscious decision to die. If God were to stand atop a mountain and say, "Die!" he would not wait for another soul to obey Him. The disciple will fall to his face and obey Him immediately. The student knows he is to die. He has read it many times. As the teacher, he has taught it many times. Yet, he hears the words and simply ignores them.

God is more than words to the disciple. God is his very being, his soul. And, the devotion the disciple has to Him is unmatched, unconditional and absolute. And, to know absolute devotion is to know God. The disciple is strict in this truth.

The student desires to learn. He sits before the teacher ready to be taught. The student says, "Teach me, master." However, the disciple stands before the master yearning to obey the commands as they are given. The disciple says, "Speak to me, master." He desires for the master to speak. He knows if he does not, then he has no life in him. Because his life is given over to God, he must literally wait for the next set of instructions before moving forward. He doesn't dare move without being told to do so.

The disciple understands that he must be disciplined. In fact, being disciplined is what makes him a disciple.

A disciple is clearly defined as one who is ready to learn. He understands that in order to learn, he must first let go of all prejudices and judgments. This one thing stumps the student. He thinks his much learning is precious, so he takes it with him to meet with God. He has the nerve to take what is foolish and compare it with what is infinite. In order for him to become the disciple, he must understand a few things. He must understand that he cannot come before God with any preconceived ideas, prideful aspirations or shady outlooks. He must come to God with no prior prejudice, no belief and no attachments. Only then can he become a disciple.

What makes the disciple so rare is that there aren't many who are willing to aspire to become one. Many are satisfied in knowing they are learning. Learning soothes them. It pats them on the back. Their great wealth of knowledge is stored with the hopes that they'll be able to use it one day before they forget it. Their knowledge has no experience. It has yet to leave the safety of their mind. It hasn't transferred to their hearts. It hasn't moved to their feet. The knowledge is stagnating. It's dying, or it's dead.

The disciple has no other aspirations of going any higher. How much higher can he go? The next step would classify him as the master. There are no steps between the disciple and the master. If the disciple was to move one step more, he'd crash right into the master. However, he steps because he understands that the process of discipleship is that of becoming a master. The disciple is wise not to start his journey that way. If he does, he'll be driven by pride rather than humility. He'll seek to overthrow the master, and we know what happens when one chooses to rebel against God. That rebel is cast from His presence.

I constantly seek to judge myself. I ask myself if I'm honestly ready for the journey. I conclude that I'll never be ready for the journey. That's the main reason why I have faith. As a disciple, I am connected to God through love; however, I step through faith. My life has been a huge journey. To say that I am ready to die would be wrong. I've already died, my friends. I stand before God ready to evaporate. I am not dying in the future. I'm already dead. My funeral took place the day I asked God to be my Lord. I no longer live. Now, the Master lives in me. Throughout this time, the Spirit of God has begun to flood me. I see myself as only the messenger assigned to give a message to those God sends me to give it to. I'm willing to travel thousands of miles to tell one man one thing at the Master's request.

Jesus, my Savior, defines for us discipleship. He was more than a student. In fact, His life and death defines the importance of what it means to be a disciple. It was in His death and resurrection that we see what it means to be a disciple. It wasn't in His teaching or His journey. It was in His death! To be a disciple is to die from your own way. It is to die from your own ability. It is to die from your own lusts. It is to die from your own cares. It means to die so that you may be resurrected.

Do you desire to be like Christ? Well, die! Die! Die! Die! Die! Leave all behind you.

WHERE ARE THE MEN?

I am oftentimes asked the question, "Where are the men?" The reason this question is asked is because of the hunger and desire for leadership, integrity, character, and humility in our society today. Turn on your local news station, and I am sure you will witness report after report of men engaging in adultery, involved in a financial scandal, arrested for battery, or a plethora of things. The list is literally endless. Women make up the majority of the local church, and many of them are single. They are watching and looking for a man to come their way in hopes he will ask her to be his bride. But, he does not come, she loses hope, and she asks the question again: "Where are the men?"

Children are sitting in single-parent home where there is a mother who is doing all she can to play the role of both father and mother, but the absence of masculinity is still felt by both the mother and the children. In their moments of heartache, the children ask the question: "Where are the men?"

The pastor sits in his office preparing the program for the next annual men's conference. The women had their conference last month, and there was not a seat left in the entire facility. However, the pastor already knows that the men's conference will have fewer numbers. On the day of the conference, the pastor urges all the men to sit in the front. By doing so, he realizes he has only enough men to fill up the first two rows in a 30-row facility. He has over 30,000 people on his attendance roll, however only 30 men came to the conference. The pastor stands up to the pulpit, grabs the microphone, and he says, "Where are the men?"

The widows sit at home alone crying because of the death of their husbands. Some sit and cry because they are hungry. They do not have anyway of getting food, and their check no longer comes to their address. One widow sits home and reads the Scripture exhorting the church to care for the widows, but she notices it is going undone. She looks outside her stained screen door with tears in her eyes, and she says, "Where are the men?"

Are you getting this now? Do you see the epidemic we have in our society today? The absence of our men is a big one. There is a massive hole in leadership for our community and our families, and the absence of men is at the center of it.

I was talking with a friend, and he began to give me figures on how many men were present in the household. I do not remember the numbers exactly, but they were not too bad; however, my eyes began to tear up. As I heard the numbers, I could only think about my father's presence in my life. See, my father was present, but he was silent. I remember praying to God one night that I would rather had not known my father than to had known him, been around him, but still yearn and desire him and his guidance because of his silence. I am overjoyed that men are agreeing to be present in the house, but my heart breaks because their presence does very little for the household. Although they are present, they are still silent. A husband and a father is responsible for more than just being present. He is tasked to guide, lead, equip, and obey. Being present is one thing—being active in your presence is another.

When I was in high school, I worked for a group, and we primarily worked in the Georgia Dome and Turner Field. On game days, the crowd would be packed with men. They were everywhere. They were willing to endure the drive from their home, the traffic, the expensive parking fees, the long way to the stadium, the crazy crowds, and the task of finding their seats. Some of the men even braved the cold or hot weather by dragging a grill and food outside so they could barbeque with some of their friends, and a couple of strangers. The men were willing to put themselves in danger, or embrace any difficulty to get to watch a game that would have no eternal value whatsoever. They are willing to do whatever was necessary to catch a firsthand glimpse of their team's victory while their family failed at home.

Like many of my friends, my father constantly worked. I rarely saw him at home. He was only off on the weekends, but I knew that his time was limited. Saturday was our grass-cutting or housework day, so I knew that day was out for some quality father-to-son bonding. Then, I had no hope in Sunday because I knew football or basketball was coming on television. I quit trying to compete with sports on television. I finally gave up, and I came to the conclusion that my father had to care more about those games than me. I was the boy who got on the baseball team to impress my father, but I only played one game then quit. I went to basketball camp, but I eventually quit it as well. Then, I decided to play football in my middle school career. I did not quit, but each game got tougher and tougher and tougher. All I wanted was for my father to come to a game. I wanted him to cheer for me like I saw him cheering for those guys he did not know on television. I realize I was not as good as those guys on television, but I just wanted my father's attention, his guidance, his presence, and his affirmation.

Like many boys, I would constantly ask my mother, "Mom, where is dad?" I needed an answer to affirm something in me and convince me that he was not just trying to stay away from me. I wanted to believe he really loved me. I wanted to believe he really cared.

Honestly, is this not the malady of our society today? Everyone desires to know the whereabouts of our men. I can tell you some of the places they congregate. They are filling up stadiums and arenas for sporting events, standing alone the sideline at PGA tours, sitting in the stands at the racing track, packed on a boat with fishing gear, waiting patiently in the woods with hunting gear, sitting in the boardroom of the company, posted up or dancing in the nightclubs, giving away their money in strip clubs, sitting in front of a computer watching pornography, hiding behind a computer screen and an image they have built on social networks, and doing amazing acts of heroism for others while their family starves and perishes at home. Finding the men is not difficult. However, we have to be sure we clearly define what kind of men we are looking for.

You may be wondering how to move towards manhood in your youth. You must take responsibility over your own growth by way of the decisions you make. Boys hand responsibility to their mothers, fathers, teachers and mentors. They seek to shift the blame in the spirit of self-preservation. But those headed toward manhood take responsibility into their own hands. They do not give in to fleshly pride; they are humble. They do not succumb to the pressures of high school; they are submitted to God. They forego their animalistic impulses, and they are not subjected to their hormones. They hold in high regard their own responsibility to manage their own flesh. They rise above. You, sir, must rise above.

The first step that you must take in your journey toward manhood is fully submitting yourself to Christ. Although the pressures of the flesh—the temptation to sleep with many girls, the struggle against drugs, reckless parties and porn—are strong, you are stronger through the power of Christ. Submit yourself to Him. Although your flesh may be weak, He is strong. Don't take pride in your own self-control; your flesh is deceitful and cannot be trusted. Humbly submit your flesh to Christ. You cannot mature by sheer will. Behavior modification only lasts so long. Instead, you must be made new by the transformation power of Jesus Christ. When you're fully submitted to Him, His Spirit will overcome your flesh. This submission to Christ is your strength. Your role in society, as a Christian youth, is to grow into a man who is Spirit-led. Under the influence of the Holy Spirit, you will lead, build and influence the community around you.

See, the world does not need heroism, big muscles, tight abs, high academic training, and a stellar resume from men. What society needs are men who are repentant, humble, and broken. It needs men who are humbly submitted to God and

His commands. It needs men who stand up for righteousness, and does not give in to sin, and those who stand up for their family by guiding their wife and children. Society does not need more brute beasts who are led by animalistic impulses. We need true followers of Christ—men of righteousness and walkers of truth. We need men of faith and those who have found their strength in Lord. This is what society needs.

Now, I have given you the places where you can find the men, but I want to share something that is a little deeper with you about the spiritual and emotional whereabouts of men. Let us begin.

The confidence of man dissipates as he continues to sin. He understands that he is a hypocrite if he chooses to speak out and against the very sinful action he understands God hates. For example, he isn't confident to speak out about the ill effects of pornography because he knowingly indulges in it hourly, daily, weekly, monthly, yearly, etc. Or, it could be that he uses drugs as a door to enter into a state of nirvana. He understands that he is a hypocrite if he speaks out against it, so he sits silently in the corner of life. He takes off his armor, which is fully detailed in Ephesians 6:10-18, and he becomes easy prey for the enemy.

Like any scavenger, the enemy stalks his prey. 1 Peter 5:8 says, "Be sober, be vigilant; because your adversary the devil, as a roaring lion, walketh about, seeking whom he may devour." One must ask, "Which prey will he seek to devour?" Another must answer, "Any prey that appears weak and feeble." Carnivores and scavengers, as much as they love to get the largest in the clan to have as food, stalk the group and prey upon the young, the feeble, and those who are unable to define themselves. Spiritually, there is no difference. We are unarmed. We have taken off our armor. Some have yet to put it on. We are ignorant of our assignments here on this planet. We do not know or are taught about the God we are asked to love, so we love amiss!

The enemy is after the weak and the feeble. Our confidence is at stake, and it is severely damaged at the presence of sin. Our confidence grows when we attain more knowledge about God, endure trials and hardships for the glory of God, and seek to walk blamelessly with the assistance of God.

We are told to flee sin and its deadly operation. We have much at stake. Lives are ready to be changed at the hands of God. The Gospel must be preached, and it takes confidence to preach it. It is easy to tell a confident man who preaches the Gospel. His words are filled with passion and conviction. It is also easy to tell a man deeply emerged in sin.

Sin separates man from God. It is because of the separation that we need Jesus Christ. If it were not for Jesus, we would still be committed to an everlasting hell. However, those who have faith in Jesus shall be given the gift of salvation, and the evidence of that salvation will be a changed heart. Once the heart is changed, the life will show proof of that change. That means the sin and evil deeds the man once loved, he will begin to hate and detest. He used to spend all night watching pornography, but the work of God's Spirit in his heart has changed his desire to watch it. Now, he sits in his closet praying for hours and building his relationship with God. The sin may knock on the door of his heart, but, unlike Cain, he will subdue it and become master over it. He will not allow sin to get into his heart and defile him. Instead, he fights valiantly against the spiritual rulers of darkness, and he flees sexual immorality.

Every man is not willing to fight, flee, or submit. Therefore, they are overrun with sin. It consumes their heart, and it shows in their life. They ignore all the warnings in Proverbs given to the son. They go into the adulteress's house even though they know her ways lead to death. They give their strength over to loose women even though they know the women will turn their heart from God. They ignore God's commands, and they have faith in self rather than having faith in God. This sin that exists in their life makes some cowards and the others prideful. The cowards are those who know the words of the Lord, but they still do not follow them. They know they should flee fornication, but they give in to it anyway. As the sun goes down and a sense of heaviness fills the boy's heart, he opens up his laptop, goes into his room, locks the door, and watches pornography as a way to relieve his stress. Or, he goes into his parent's medicine cabinet, grabs some drugs, and takes them to give him a momentary high so he may escape his momentary low. He is the one who is sending the sexually explicit messages to others, an active member on meet-up sites, a regular at the local pub, and a buyer of music that promotes lust and violence. He knows what he is doing is wrong, and it affects him. The sin makes him a coward, so he sits in darkness practicing evil while knowing what he is doing is wrong. What does a coward do? A coward hides. A coward hides in darkness, and lives in rebellion. He may go to church, but he sits in the back where he is not seen. He is too ashamed to pray or proclaim the truth because he knows his life is a lie. He gets so comfortable in his sin that learns to live a cowardly life. He lives a plastic life where he is cowering inside. He is a coward.

The other man is like the coward; however, he has grown prideful in his sin. He sits in the front row of the church clapping, dancing, and shouting. There is no true repentance in him. He hears the word of God as it is preached in the temple, but it does not enter his heart. He does not care that he is turning the grace of God into lasciviousness. He gives excuses as to why his heart is hard and cold towards God. He gives more excuses as to why he sins. He does not see the problem in going to the clubs on Friday night and singing and shouting in the choir on Sunday morning. He does not see the importance of being the same man on Saturday night that he is on Sunday morning. He is rebellious and cold-hearted. He becomes so bold that he begins to justify his sin using Scripture. He gets to such a point that he no longer cares who knows about his sin. Instead, he makes it public. He freely jokes and laughs about his mistress to the other deacons. He freely pours up alcohol and lights a blunt when he is in front of the pastor. His heart is cold, and he is as prideful as he could ever be.

Both the coward and the prideful man are in rebellion. Neither one of them are following the commands of God. You can look around our society today and see exactly what I am saying. The cowards only come out at night when the light has gone so they can be mischievous and sinful. John 3:20 reads, "For everyone who does evil hates the light, and does not come to the light, lest his deeds should be exposed." The prideful go out in the day, and they go out at night. There rebellion has been amplified to such a point that they no longer care what anyone things—including God. They freely leave their wife and children to indulge in sin. Their rebellion is deep, and their heart is full of sin.

While at a book signing in Columbia, Missouri, I sat down with a group of guys who were leading a Christian male group on their college campus. The leader of the group asked me a question that has been asked for years and years and years. He asked, "Cornelius, how do we get the men to come out?" They told me about an event they had where they had food, and the event was totally free. Considering the fact it is a college campus, they figured food would lure the men out for the events. However, that was not the case. The guy told me only a few guys showed up for the event. He told me they passed out flyers, did announcements, and did everything within their power to get the guys to come out to the event; however, none of it worked. They tried to analyze the difference between why guys would go to sporting events in mass numbers but would not take one hour to sit and be taught the Word of God. After hearing this, God began to deal with me about this issue. My brain could not comprehend why the men were not coming either. I had to take this matter to God in prayer. This was the outcome of my prayer time and what I shared with those guys: **People will go where their heart leads them**. Let me explain this to you.

The heart is the center of man. It is the matrix for which all things flow. Luke 6:45 reads, "The good man out of the good treasure of his heart brings forth what is good; and the evil man out of the evil treasure brings forth what is evil; for his mouth speaks from that which fills his heart." A mouth filled with filthy communication means that his heart is filled with filth. Have you ever been around someone who listened to so much hateful, lustful music? Do you remember how they talked after they listened to it and what came out of their mouth? If they listened to lustful music all day long, you could only expect for them to say and do lustful things because it lust had filled their heart. They spent time meditating on that lustful song, and it soon began to take over their heart. This is a principle I never want you to forget. **Whatever you meditate on the most is what you will worship.** Meditating on lust will guarantee that you will definitely serve lust. The same is true for everything else. This is why Joshua says, "This book of the law shall not depart from your mouth, but you shall meditate on it day and night, so that you may be careful to do according to all that is written in it; for then you will make your way prosperous, and then you will have success" in Joshua 1:8. Joshua stresses the importance of meditating on the Word of God. Such meditating will ensure success because the meditation will grow your faith in God.

I am sure the men on that college campus were meditating on their exams and too preoccupied with worldly matters to even consider anything spiritual. The yearning of the heart is so serious that not even a necessity for life, which is the offering of food for the conference, was enough to draw the men there. It was not that the men did not have time to go to the conference. They could have made or found the time. Anytime someone says they do not have time to do something, you should call them a liar. Their issue is not time. Their issue is desire. If they truly desired to be there, they would have found the time. They would have done whatever they needed to do to be there for that event. They did not have the desire to be there because their heart was polluted with sin.

You may read this and say, "Well, how do we change their heart?" Honestly, you cannot change the heart of a man. Only God can change a man's heart and bring him to repentance. You can change his actions, but you cannot change his heart. Man is like a lion. A lion eats meat naturally. He is a savage beast who roams, seeks, and devours whatever he wants. If you throw a lion in a cage with just grass and hay, he will starve to death. Why? It is because he eats meat. It is in his nature to eat meat. He needs it to survive. You can teach the lion how to jump through rings of fire, dance around a circus, or take pictures with children, but you cannot teach him how to eat grass. Trying to get him to eat grass is trying to change his nature. Man cannot do it. Man can changes the actions of the beast, but only God can change his nature.

The same is true for man. I can sit down with a boy, and I could teach him how to be a "good" churchgoer. I could teach him how to sit in the church, how to sing in the choir, how to give in the offering, how to stand and shout at the right time of the message, how to pray according to selfish desires instead of God's will, and how to even stand behind a pulpit and talk as if what he is saying is true. I could teach him how to be a great churchgoer, but all those things could still send him to hell because his heart was not changed. God did not have his heart. He was a son of the devil although he perfected the Christian clichés and has all the external things down.

The men on the campus are like men all over the world. Their heart is not right. So, we try to do all of these things to try to appeal to men, but they do not work because their heart is not in the hands of God. They are quick to run to the clubs even though have to pay a cover charge. They are quick to run to the strip club or sit at home and watch pornography even though the shame and ruin if they are found out is great. However, they are not willing to sit in a free conference to be taught about the Lord's commands. That is not an issue of advertising. It is an issue of the heart.

Now, the only logical question to ask from this point is: "What should we do?" This is the question the guys asked me. I want you to turn to Acts 2. I want you to read the chapter then return back to the book.

You should have noticed a couple of things in the chapter. First, you recognize the setting is on the Day of Pentecost. The disciples were in the upper room praying like their were told to do by Christ. While praying, a rushing wind descended upon them and filled them with the Holy Spirit. Everyone thought they were drunk with wine because they were speaking in unknown tongues. Then, Peter stands up to preach in verse fourteen. Peter preaches a mighty prayer, and there was a powerful outcome. In verse 37, it reads that the crowd of people was pierced to the heart by what they heard. Then, they asked, "What shall we do?" Peter replied, "Repent, and let each of you be baptized in the name of Jesus Christ for the forgiveness of your sins; and you shall receive the gift of the Holy Spirit."

The people continued to gather together, and verse 47 reads, "...And the Lord was adding to their number day by day those who were being saved." I want you to notice the progression. The men did not start off by preaching. I do not you to think the answer to the question is preaching alone. Preaching is a part of the answer, but it is not the whole answer. Notice what the disciples did before they preached. They PRAYED! They gave themselves over to prayer until the power of God fell on them. Then, once the power of God was present, Peter preached. Because of the presence of God's power, the people's hearts were pierced by what they heard. This led to change in their lives. This was a time of transformation, and it cannot be ignored. The disciples did not go around handing out pamphlets, getting on radio shows, putting out mass messages on social media mainly because they did not have any of that stuff. What they had was prayer, and it was sufficient. I am in no way insinuating that media is wrong entirely, but it is wrong when it takes precedence over prayer.

I instructed the young leaders on that campus to pray. Then, once the presence of God hits them, preach, and preach hard with conviction.

You might ask, "Well, how will they get the men to come to their events?" Let me ask you this: Who is to say the men are obligated to go to their outings? Why can those guys not go to them? Also, you must understand that the Scriptures did not say that the disciples added to the number of those who were in attendance. Instead, it was the Lord who added to the numbers daily. We are trying to come up with gimmicks and plans and programs to make men be good fathers, be good churchgoers, be good community leaders. Those gimmicks will only last for so long. If you use carnal bait to catch them, they will expect carnal bait to keep them there. The men will not come, sit, learn, and actively participate until we pray. We need God's power, not man's ability.

So, where are the men? They are lost in the maze of this world. They have no destination, so they are willing to take whatever assignment that is placed in their hands. They are concerned about the matters of the world more than they are the matters of eternity. Nonetheless, I would not want you to think all men are this way. They are not. There are men today who have standards and are true followers of our Lord. They give themselves to devotion and prayer, and they are quick to run towards responsibility instead of running away from it. They have repentant hearts, and their life shows the change in their heart. They are not posers like some. I know you are familiar with the posers. Those are the men who hide behind their personality because they fear being exposed as an impostor. They have to force themselves into a masculine image that soon transforms them into lawless beasts instead of repentant sheep. They try to give off the appearance of being busy to give the illusion that they are needed. They fake their way through life, only pick battles they are sure to win, only accept adventures they are sure to handle, and only pursue a beauty they are sure to rescue. They are the men who are quick to speak of their heartfelt "change" and devotion to Christ while cementing the fact they are "only human." While this idea is true, many only provide such a response so they can create a way of escape just in case they attempt to steer a woman in a direction of sex and lustful conversation. They use their human frailty as an excuse and a crutch. Beware of those men.

Nevertheless, a man must know he is a man or he will forever try to prove he is one while shrinking from anything that might reveal he is not one. Ask a man this question: Do you think you are a man? Then, ask him: Why do you think you are a man? Most men are either haunted by the question or crippled by the answer. Men search for a way to escape their reality. Pornography gives them a way of escape from feeling as if they are a failure, and it can provide them with a sense of acceptance. It gives them power and control even if it is over an image on a computer screen. It allows for a man to be master over a controlled slave that does not ignore him, rebuke him, defy him, challenge him, or deny his advances, no matter how shallow he may feel inside.

Many women see the frailty in a man, and they seek to change him. If she does not succeed in changing him, then she will nag him. If nagging does not work, she will seek to become the man that she does not think he is. She might think that he's uninvolved in child-rearing, so after being unsuccessful with nagging, she begins to take matters into her own hands by disciplining her children more harshly. She might think that he's a lazy budgeter, so after exhausting her nagging, she decides to wear the pants in the relationship by making all of the financial decisions in the household without him. Instead of encouraging her husband to grow by allowing him room to lead, she leads instead. By doing so, she emasculates him. She takes cutting shears to his scrotum, and effeminates the man. She does not understand that he is looking for a partner, NOT a coach; a wife, NOT mother. But, some women feel they are forced because the only men they know are men who are inept in leading, perverse in their thinking, and immature in their living. They see that the man does not really want a wife; instead, he wants a chef, a maid, and a prostitute.

In sum, the man's heart is polluted with sin; therefore, he is going to the places where his heart leads him. Unfortunately, for many men, that place is not the church. What must we do? We must pray.

THE MAN & HIS RELATIONSHIPS

Many, many years ago I wrote a very interesting entry in my journal, and I want to share it with you. Here is the entry.

"In this life that I live, I must stop to ask if I am truly who I say that I am. Am I only a product of my surroundings? Have people, books, and words shaped this era I call life? It is at this time that I meditate on the love of people. The musk of friendship is invading this world I call my own, and it is because of past mistakes and failures that I have lost all confidence in people. Do not get me wrong. I believe people have the ability to do all that they set their minds to do. The question lies in if they actually will do it. In my own mind and in my own words I shall explain it like this:

1. *Never tell people what they need to hear. In doing so, they may never listen again to your words. But, if you must be different, tell them out of love and with time. For, your words can be as morsels of honey or as rough as sandpaper.*
2. *Never tell the full truth to those you call your friends, but if you must be totally honest, be*

honest always. Give no room for doubt or worrying. Your love is too important to that person.

3. Never give your friend your life. He may take it for ransom, only to abuse it; but if you must, give yourself away to those you love. Give all. Love has no ends; therefore, love can never be measured.

4. Never cry in front of your friends. But, if you must, shed a tear and cry out to God to increase your capacity to love that person more than you ever have before.

5. Never give gifts to those you call your friends. But, if you must, give the gift of an ear. Your words will help to shape his life, and your ear will help for those spoken words to be heard. A true friend anticipates your words and longs for your ear.

6. Never converse with those you call your friends. But, if you must, talk to them for days about things that matter. Discuss with them the internal things of life like character, heart, integrity, and change. It is in those conversations that many of those you refer to as friends will disqualify themselves.

7. Don't and never waste your time treating those known as your friends as people. They are probably shallow anyway. But, if you must, treat them like royalty. Shower and bestow love and its many bounties on them.

In many relationships you choose to build, build on love. If you want a fail-proof plan to having friends forever, love all converse with man, but befriend and confide in a few. And, if you desire for *the rest of the world to know God, perfect and show love through Him."*

That was my entry on friendship. I've grown since that post years and years ago. I see some things in it that I wouldn't say today; however, I wanted to share it with you. There are some things written that are totally valid, especially the part about love. Even so, I want to set the record straight concerning friendships.

I live in the Western portion of the hemisphere, and our culture is different from a lot of the Eastern culture, especially pertaining to friendships. Scripturally, one of the greatest examples of friendship is between David and Jonathon. Refer to 1 Samuel 18. Both David and Jonathon shared something special with one another. No, it wasn't a bed. No, it wasn't a woman. They shared intimacy with one another. Yes, I know "intimacy" isn't a word that you would normally see associated with two men; however, I need you to understand that their relationship was not culturally-bound like most male-to-male relationships are in the West. Let's be honest for a moment—most people use the word "friend" very loosely. Oftentimes, people consider others friends who they've only encountered on a couple of occasions. They assume others they've never met as friends just because they know them from the Internet or social networking sites. I've even met people who have told me that they felt like I was their friend because they have read my tweets or posts on Facebook.

Sadly, most people don't have any true friends. They may know a lot of people, but they have few friends. I have reached my max on Facebook for friends; however, I have very few friends. I have thousands and thousands of followers, but I have few friends. I cannot deceive myself into thinking all those people are actually my friends, and I pray you don't deceive yourself either.

I want you to take a very close look at friendship. I want you to evaluate your circle of friends to decide whether or not you've made a wise decision concerning those you call your friends. Do they motivate you to righteousness, or push you further into damnation?

There's much to be said about friendship. We all desire friends. These are people we can trust, depend on, rely on, communicate with, cry with, build with, laugh with, etc. Our constant struggle for friendship oftentimes leaves us broken and without the very relationship we struggle to attain—a great friendship.

The friendship between David and Jonathon, a son of King Saul, is a beautiful representation of loyalty, honor, and respect. Jonathon risked his own life for his friend's sake. This type of union doesn't happen every day in our society, especially seeing how selfish and prideful many can be. Neither David nor Jonathon were concerned about each other's wealth, trying to get each other involved in business schemes, or attempting to see what they could take from each other. The *friendship was based on mutual submission*, which is a byproduct of true love.

Having a relationship like David and Jonathon could be a very risky thing; however, it is well-worth it in the end. We must understand that *love* is the foundation for a great friendship. Also, there must be *transparency*. A friendship should be a safe haven from the rest of the world. The very presence of a friend should provide comfort and peace. A great friendship is so honest that it allows for a great deal of judgement. Friends give one another an opportunity to correct one another in love. They sharpen one another for the health of the relationship.

I would encourage you to *evaluate those you refer to as friends.* Understand that the word "friend" is an honorable word. It is a title that should not be bestowed on just anyone. It is one that should be earned. Jesus said, "You are my friends if you do what I command" (John 15:14). Notice the restriction He places on friendship. He **did not make it all-inclusive**. The requirement is clearly stated. Make sure your requirements are biblical, righteous, just and fair.

Lastly, be the friend you desire to have in others. *Show yourself friendly.* Reach out to that person you look up to and greatly respect. Start a conversation. Don't be afraid to make friends with people who do not look or act like you. The diversity will be a great thing because it will cause you to grow and mature. Be sure your circle is filled with people who are focused on maturing. Honestly, you can't be sharpened by a dull blade, and you'll cut yourself playing around with a sharp one.

Now, this is should be a very interesting chapter. We have dealt with your relationship with God and with friends. Now, I want to deal primarily with your relationships with the opposite sex. I want you to know my story so you have an idea of where I'm coming from concerning relationships.

I've had very few girlfriends in my lifetime. I began "dating" in the fifth grade. I called it dating, but I didn't have a clue what I was doing. I remember writing a letter to her while sitting in class. The letter was like any letter a fifth grader would write. It asked if she liked me. She would indicate whether she did or did not by checking either the "yes" or "no" box. I didn't include a "maybe" box because I didn't think it was valid. I figured she should know, and that was that. I had one of my classmates to give her the letter. As the day was ending, I headed to the bus to go home. One of my classmates ran up to me to hand me back the letter. I was so nervous. My stomach was tightening up, and I could barely breath. I sat down on the bus, and I slowly opened the letter. To my amazement, she marked the "yes" box. To me, that meant that we were practically married. You have to remember that I was still in elementary school. We never spent any time together. Neither one of us could drive, and I didn't have a clue where she lived. We didn't talk on the phone, either. It was a very dysfunctional relationship. We had to finally end the relationship after a meeting my grandmother had with her grandparents. As it turned out, she was my cousin. Yes, she was my cousin. She was a distant cousin, but she was still my cousin. Needless to say, we stopped talking from that point forward.

My relationships with the opposite sex declined greatly. I was very insecure about my weight. I hated the way that I looked, and there were times when I just wanted to die. I would see the men on the television, and I wanted so badly to look like them. I wanted to have smooth, curly hair, so I would buy those texturizing perms in the box. I used those for awhile until I almost burned my scalp off my head. I was told that the longer you leave it on your head, the better it would make your hair. I chose to leave it on about 5 minutes longer than what the instructions on the box said. I'm sure I suffered second-degree burns from it. It was painful just to wash it out of my hair. I wanted to have the six-pack abs, so I started doing whatever I thought would give me some. I would do sit-ups and run a little every now and then. I didn't do anything consistently, though. As time went on, I started to give up. I figured I'd remain that short, fat boy for the rest of my life. I would lay down to watch television with my plate sitting on my stomach. I'd eat every kind of sugary snack you threw at me. I had given up completely, and I figured it was okay to do so.

After moving to Georgia, I met two very different women. I considered one to be a friend, and I was quickly falling for the other one. The one I considered a friend was there to listen when I talked. She was understanding, and she didn't seem overly-emotional, so I thought. I felt like I could just talk to her. I thought the other girl was pretty. I wanted to get to know her more. I wanted her to see me the same way I saw her, so I would say little things to her in class. I would bring her gifts on certain holidays. I would get her food from the cafeteria when she requested it. I was absolutely smitten over her. Finally, the last day of school came, and there I was ready to make my move. We were talking about what she had planned to do over the summer. I looked at her, and I asked her if she was willing to go to the movies with me. She looked at me, and she told me that she didn't think that was going to happen. She told me that she didn't date my type of guys. I asked her what "type" that was. She said, "fat guys." Yes, I was heartbroken! I was already self-conscious of my weight, and her words made me feel ten times worse. I wanted to find a rock to crawl under and never come out. I went home, locked my bedroom door, pushed my bed against the wall, and I began to do pushups. I was tired of playing the victim. I was going to do something about my weight. That summer, I went to the gym 5 to 6 times a week. I changed my entire eating habits. I lost almost 55 pounds. I went from a size 44-waist to a 32-wasit. I felt like a new man when I entered back into those high school doors for my tenth-grade school year. People didn't even recognize me. They thought I was a new kid. Immediately, I saw the girl who I was smitten over sitting at the table with some of her friends. I walked up to her, and I noticed that she had gotten heavier over the summer. She looked at me, and she said, "Wow, Antonio, [that is my middle name] you have lost so much weight." I looked back at her, and I said, "Yeah, and I see you found it." That was the beginning of a very dark time in my life. My sarcasm was a clear indication that I was still hurting on the inside. Even though I looked different on the outside, I was still that same hurting, wretched person within.

JUST FRIENDS

Through all of that, the other girl and I were still friends. She knew about the entire thing. We talked every day of the summer, and she was well aware of my desire to lose weight. As years continued, my relationship with her also went sour. I thought we could be just friends, but I was wrong. There was time when our conversation was deep and very intimate. I was telling her things that no one else knew. She knew a side of me that I wouldn't share with anyone else. I was doing what many men think is okay to do. I was using her to hear me when I wanted to vent, and be there when I wanted someone to talk to. I was a form of abuse. I didn't realize one great truth, and I want to make sure you know and understand it: **You learn to adore what continues to feed you**. When you were a baby, you cried and screamed because you were hungry. You desperately needed food to eat. Your guardian made sure you had food, and you learned to adore him or her for it. The same is true for sin. We run after sin because we are hungry for it. We get the idea in our heads that it is feeding the desire that we longed to have fulfilled. Soon enough, we learn to adore the sin so much that we refuse to turn away from it even when we know death is inevitable because of it. Most men are fed by pornography. It feeds the lust that exists in their heart, and they learn to adore it even with the risk that it could ruin their lives forever. This same principle applies to our friendships. See, I was giving her something that she grew to adore. I was giving her intimacy. No, I didn't have sex with her. To think sex is the beginning of intimacy is wrong anyway. I gave her myself by giving her my words in conversation. My words, and your words, flow out of your heart. She cannot dive into my heart to see the words. I must give them to her. I must share them with her, and that is what I did. I gave her my words from my heart. That is intimacy. I allowed her into me so that she could see what was inside. She learned to adore it. You know what happened next, right? Yes, she told me how she felt about me. She was in love with me. I quickly had to cut off the idea of being in a relationship with her because I didn't feel the same way. I finally realized that I was using her, and I was destroying her heart in the meantime. She was thinking that there was a possibility of a relationship because I was willing to give her my words; however, I just wanted to vent. This helped me to see that there was no way I could enter into a friendship with the opposite sex. Every time I tried to do it, it ended the same way. Either I began to adore her, or she began to adore me. Foolishly, we didn't see what was really going on. We began to adore the intimacy that we shared with one another. Sir, intimacy is to be reserved for your wife, not some random girl who you call a friend. If you want a friend, find another man. Allow him to sharpen you, admonish you, rebuke you, and hear you.

THE BROTHERHOOD

I would even go as far as advising you to find three types of men in your life. First, there is the man you're able to look up to. This is the man who advises you in everyday life. He may be skilled in business or interpersonal relations. He should be sound in Biblical doctrine. He should be a husband to one wife. She should live above reproach. His example should be worthy of emulation. His words should match his actions. His family should respect him, and his household should be in order. He should be able to help you in different stages of life. I have many of these kinds of men in my life. Many of them have changed over the years. They simply disqualified themselves, and I no longer listen to some of them. However, there are some I still respect highly. I treasure their words, but I do not place their words before God's words. That is a fatal mistake, and it is one that many men, especially in the church, are falling into today. Men begin to place a man on a pedestal so much so that their words become greater than God's words. Their life becomes all about what the "mentor" says instead of what God says. I've been in that kind of abusive relationship. I had a preacher ask me a question that immediately caused me to rethink my entire relationship with him. He asked, "How does it feel to know you are doing something that you said 'God said,' yet I disagree with?" I was very straight in telling him that I was going to do what God said even if he disagreed. God said it; therefore, I didn't need his agreement on the matter. I've never looked back from that day forth. It is important that you are deft in hearing the voice of the Lord so that you are not rebellious for the sake of flesh. Practice hearing God's voice by spending quality time with Him every day, and studying the Bible on a regular basis. Without the Word of God, you are able to be led astray by the voice of a stranger. The more time you spend in prayer and reading the Bible, the more skilled you will become in discerning His instructions from your desires. Understand that I believe in wise counsel. I believe in the knowledge that comes from more seasoned veterans; however, I will never allow their words to supersede the words of God. Let's be honest. Most of the older men of our day have had longer to complicate the very simplicity of life. Their knowledge is as stale as year-old bread. I wouldn't let most of the older men today guide me across a 1-inch deep river because their advice is loaded with error and man's thinking. Nonetheless, I'd advise you to begin to pray about finding a seasoned man who can advise you during life's toughest and priciest moments. I am that man for many young men, and it is no easy feat. However, the payoff is well-worth it.

Secondly, you need to find a man who you can look straight to. This man is usually someone around your age or maturity level. I don't have many friends who are around my age level. I befriend older men because I feel as if we have more to relate with. I run several businesses, I am author of several books, I am pastor of a church, I am married, I have a child, etc. I'm not interested in when the next set of shoes are coming out. My primary goal of the year isn't to get to the new game console that allows you to control it with your brain. I'm focused on the future. My desires have changed. Before I was married, I related a lot with single men. I was able to befriend them because we had so much in common. Then I got married. Now that I'm married, I don't talk to my single friends much. I have a few, but our conversation is very surface-level. I converse mostly with my married friends. They're able to relate to things that I'm saying. Now that my child is born, I love talking to my friends who are married with children. They really relate to what's going on. These men are able to look me in my face and encourage me, admonish me, and rebuke me. We help one another. This kind of relationship is seen between David and Jonathan. They held each other accountable. They were there for one another. I oftentimes ask myself if David, when he became king, would've pursued Bathsheba if Jonathan were alive. I really don't think so. I think Jonathan would have pushed David to join his army in battle. I think

Jonathan would've been there to keep King David accountable because, honestly, he had no one there to keep him accountable. All the men of David's army looked up to him. He was the king, and that is no easy position to hold. The king shouldn't be seen taking advice from the solider. Kind David needed a friend to tell him what he was doing was wrong and to keep him accountable. Because King David had no one there to keep him accountable, God sent the prophet Nathan to rebuke him. God didn't send a solider. The king could've turned away the soldier, or better yet, just had him killed. God sent someone who could look King David in the eyes and tell him "...thus says the Lord!" We need men like that in our lives who can tell us to stop watching pornography, tell us to stay out of that bed, and tell us to pursue righteousness. This is your accountability partner.

Thirdly, and lastly, you need men who can look up to you. I don't know if you realize this, but we have a tendency to do better when we know others are watching and depending on us. As I stated above, I have many men who look up at me as an example for them. That is a heavy responsibility, but it is one that I cannot afford to waste. You may think that there aren't any men who would look up to you, but you would be amazed. Someone is always looking at you, especially those in your house. You cannot afford to live in sin. I cannot afford to live in sin. I realize many people are drawn to Christ because of my holy living. I am an ambassador of Christ. You are an ambassador of Christ. An ambassador carries a very important message and represents a foreign government or sovereign body. You represent a greater good that far exceeds this temporal world. Your conduct should be mature, your conversation should be convicting, your thoughts should be pure, and your life should be worth emulating. You should be able to tell others to follow you as you follow Christ. You should resist temptation, flee sexual immorality, and turn from all ungodliness. You should rise with a greater awareness that doesn't revolve around you. It should revolve around your pursuit towards Christlikeness; thereby, allowing other men to follow you. Your words and your actions shouldn't lead men to you—they should lead men to God. Sir, you need others to pour into. You need others to follow you. You need to know that you are an example to others. You need to know that you are not a mistake. You are an ambassador of Christ, so act like one.

RELATIONSHIPS WITH THE OPPOSITE SEX

Let's go back to what I was writing earlier about my relationship with the other woman. The first relationship I mentioned was meant to be an intimate one. Actually, they both were pretty intimate. However, I wanted to actually pursue the first woman in a romantic relationship. I wanted to be exclusively hers. I didn't even realize that I wasn't really ready for a relationship. I thought I was, but I wasn't. I didn't have anyone to sit me down and talk to me about being in a relationship. The only advice I got was from an uncle who told to "chase that rabbit." Yes, he used the word "rabbit" to refer to a vagina. I really don't know what he meant by it, so don't feel bad if you don't either. I wrote a blog entry about when you should enter into a relationship. I want to share it with you:

"I am oftentimes asked the question: *"When should I enter into a relationship?"* People want to know when is the most opportune time. They want to know if it is when you feel like you are "in love" with someone. Is it when you feel like you want to be married? Is it when you feel a deep longing to have someone so you won't be lonely? What is it? When should you begin looking to be in a relationship?

I am not sure if you are going to like this answer, but the truth is sometimes a very hard pill to swallow. **You should enter into a relationship with the opposite sex when you are ready for marriage.** What does that mean? Let me explain it for you. A man (<u>notice I did not say boy</u>) should enter into a relationship with a woman (<u>notice I did</u>

not say girl) when *they are both prepared* and *ready* to engage one another in a marriage covenant. The man should begin showing **fruit of his masculinity**. He will *show fruit of responsibility, honor, trust, respect, humility, love, sacrifice, hard work, patience, joy*, etc. The boy differs from the man because the boy is lazy, disrespectful, rude, impatient, wrathful, unwilling to sacrifice, selfish, etc. The boy chooses to buy new shoes or a new video game instead of paying his bills. *Many girls marry the boy thinking they can change him.* They also think it is fun to marry a "*bad boy*." Sadly, *bad boys make bad husbands and bad fathers.* Unfortunately, they cannot change an unregenerate man's heart. **Only God** can change that man and produce fruit that wasn't able to be produced before. *The boy makes excuses instead of making things happen*. The boy needs a human to be close around to make sure he is doing what he needs to do, but the man can be trusted to do the job he's been assigned with little to no supervision. *The woman will show fruit of humility, submission, honor, virtue, loyalty, modesty, wisdom, hard work, etc.* The girl is more focused on going to the party or buying a new handbag instead of using her time to care for her home. *The woman puts away childish things, and directs her focus to becoming more motherly, charitable, honorable, and respectable*. She doesn't desire a "bad boy" because she's focused on serving our good, holy God.

The man and the woman should begin to show fruit of their maturity. Then, and only then, are they truly ready to engage the opposite sex for a relationship. Does this mean both the man and woman are perfect when they begin the relationship? Absolutely not. However, it does mean **they are working towards perfection by maturing and allowing godly fruit to produce within them**. They abstain from sexual immorality, turn away from temptation, and honor God instead of their flesh. Salvation can be seen in their life by the fruit that is produced within them through and by their faith in Jesus Christ.

On the other hand, a boy and girl engage in a relationship for **recreation**. It is *immature fun* for them. That is why they treat it as if it has no importance. They will cheat on one another. They will lie to one another. They will mislead one another simply because they either have no focus, no true purpose, and/or no fruit of maturity. They do what children do, which is, *do whatever they think is right to do*.

My wife and I firmly stand by the tradition of courting. We believe *guardians should be an intricate part of the relationship.* The *relationship should have boundaries*, and *it should be treated with respect*. Children will not understand these truths. They will rebel, and they will seek to do what is in their own heart. So many marriages are destroyed today because two children decided to engage themselves in a relationship that is purposed for mature adults. Also, it hurts my heart to hear about a married couple who despise the children they birth. Honestly, why in the blue moon did they get married? **Marriage is the institution purposed for reproducing children and raising those children in the fear and instruction of the Lord**. If you do not want children or to honor God with the production of children, then please reconsider getting into a relationship. *Your job, feelings, and all that other stuff should not take precedence over the established purpose of marriage.* Again, children will not understand this truth, and their irresponsibility will lead them straight to ruin.

Simply put, **if you do not show fruit of biblical maturity, if you're not ready for children, or if you're not ready to honor your spouse or God, please do not get in a relationship**. *Do not take someone on the journey with you if you know in your heart that it will have a dead end.* Let your life show fruit of your maturity. Seek to honor God in your singleness, and be passionately sold out to Him until a spouse has been presented to you. Consider these things as you continue your journey of life."

I hope that opened your eyes and allowed you to have a fresh perspective on relationships. When I finally entered into my courtship with Heather, my now-wife, I knew I had to do things differently than I how I did them in the past. I made a vow to God not to kiss my wife until we were married. I was able to keep that vow. I finally kissed her one-year-and-eight-months after the first day we met, on our wedding day. That moment was special, but it was not cheap. It cost something. It was valuable. I had to have boundaries in my relationship. Here are some of the things I did.

1. **We didn't get too close**. You're probably thinking, "what's too close, huh?" You know what's too close. If you were standing in front of a fire, the heat radiating from the blaze would indicate that you're too close. The

same is true for relationships—when you're too close to someone, you will have some indications. Usually, you will get an erection or this euphoric, lustful feeling will consume you. I didn't need for Heather to get close to me. I already knew my equipment worked. I didn't need to test it out. We didn't give each other chest-to-chest hugs. We didn't rub and touch on each other. We kept our space, and we made sure it remained respectful.

2. **We didn't cuddle**. I met so many men who come to me to tell me how they ended up having sex with their girlfriend. It's never an accident. It's not like their clothes just came off of them by osmosis. It was premeditated, or planned out. Usually, the beginnings of the sexual adventure starts out with cuddling. It seems innocent, but it brings on an entirely new set of temptations. You're lying there on one another, and the temptation to touch increases. It's just wise to stay away from it altogether.

3. **We weren't alone**. I don't want you to take this as if Heather and I were never by ourselves. We actually rode in the car alone. We actually sat at my home alone before a couple of hours. We even sat at dinner alone. We just didn't do it independently of anyone else. We made sure someone always knew where we were and what we were doing. When we went out, it was mostly with other couples. We would spend time laughing and enjoying each other in groups. We still had fun, but it was in a controlled environment. We didn't seek to be alone and out of

communication with anyone. We didn't go to late-night movies because of the temptation. We made a decision to never do anything independently of anyone else, and it helped us in the end.

I'm sure there are many more. I encourage you to get my book <u>So, You Want to be Married?</u> I give very detailed information about my entire courting relationship in that book.

Ultimately, there's one message I want you to receive: As the man, I advise you to shoulder the responsibility of maintaining the purity of the relationship. Don't allow for things to happen that you know could be avoided. If the temptation is there, flee it. If you have to call someone to assist so something doesn't happen, do it. If you realize that she's coming on to you, RUN! Be a man, not a hypocrite!

Your relationship with the opposite sex should be a mirror image of your relationship with Christ. Count the cost before pursuing that woman. Make sure you can adequately fulfill the request of being a husband and a father. This is not an area of your life you should take lightly; therefore, be wise.

WHERE ARE WE GOING?

Brother, I don't know about you, but I'm tired of empty rhetoric; we don't need more preachers hooping and hollering about superficial things. I'm tired of useless arguing; we don't need any more banter about whether or not women must wear pants in church. I'm tired of pretentious hypocrites; we don't need more pastors cursing out of the same mouth they bless with. I am tired of excuses and laziness being the reason why nothing is being done in the home or in the community.

Honestly, we have more truth than what we are willing to obey. We are already entrenched in denominational traditions, marketing strategies, and self-promoting ventures that serve no real eternal purpose. Nowadays, everyone has a plan, a business, or a strategy for success. Unfortunately, most times, none of it centers on the spreading of the Gospel. There are so many people who are talking about what is wrong with the Church; however, there are very few who are actually passionate about making a true, lasting difference and being purposeful about spreading the Gospel truth.

Let me ask you a series of serious questions that I pray cause you to ponder. Have you given your life fully to Christ? Is He truly your Lord and Savior? If so, then when is the last time you shared Christ with someone? When is the last time you tried? Where is your passion? Where is your purpose? Why are you living? What are you doing with your life? What are your excuses? Why are you not busy about the things of God?

I oftentimes hear about the success of Olympic athletes. Some of them begin training when they are young. They go without worldly pleasantries that many say they cannot live without. They refuse to date or have any relationship that could deter them from one day obtaining the gold medal. They forgo eating unhealthy meals. They become disciplined and live structured lives. They do all of this just so they could one day obtain a gold medal that serves no eternal value. It is a gold medal that is capable of being ruined. Many sit back and watch these athletes as they compete for the highest prizes; however, very few realize the work, sacrifice, and passion that were involved in making their possibility a reality. Ponder this for a moment. How is it that these athletes could sacrifice so much only for gold that will one day fade and tarnish? If they can do it for a gold medal that will tarnish and fade then how much more can we do for an eternal crown that will never fade or tarnish? Paul writes in 1 Corinthians 9:24-27, "Do you not know that those who run in a race all run, but only one receives the prize? Run in such a way that you may win. Everyone who competes in the games exercises self-control in all things. They then do it to receive a perishable wreath, but we an imperishable. Therefore I run in such a way, as not without aim; I box in such a way, as not beating the air; but I discipline my body and make it my slave, so that, after I have preached to others, I myself will not be disqualified." Take time to ponder this truth. Then, take time to review your life.

I want you to consider your passion and your purpose for living. I also want you to consider your distractions. Ask yourself what is distracting you from fulfilling the task God has given you to do. Is it school, work, Internet, television, or other extracurricular activities? Are you fully engaged in what God has destined for you, or are you clearly meandering through life with no real purpose or passion? Sir, I can assure you that you can get so much accomplished if you take time to turn off the television, power-off the game systems, turn off the cell phone, and forgo an evening out with your buddies. That book God has told you to write, that property He has told you to clean, that place He has told you to visit, and the life He has called you to live should not be placed on hold any longer! Get rid of the distractions, and be free from your addictions. Pedophilia and pornography is running rampant in our society. Nowadays, there is no telling what you will see on television. I do not know what you deal with in your life, but I ask that you do not hide it any longer. Drop the fig leaves, reveal your addictions, understand that you have a problem, and confess and believe that Jesus Christ has set you free from your addiction(s). Jesus has set you free from the bondage of sin. He did what you and I could not do! Therefore, be free, brother.

Consider this. Consider sitting in jail fully chained from head to toe. All of the sudden you hear the sound of keys rattling. That sound of rattling keys gives you hope. The sound gets closer, and closer, and closer to your cell. Then, the door flies open, the chains fall off, and you are set free from your bondage. How great of a moment would that be for you? However, that is not the case is it? There is little-to-no excitement about our freedom from the bondage of sin, is there? Instead, we choose to sit in the jail cell while the door is wide open. The truth is that we do not want to let go of our addictions. We know the door is open. We know the chains are gone, but we will not let go of the sin. Brother, be free so you can be passionate with purity.

Oftentimes, we fail to realize and we live to forget that we will face our holy God one day. What will we have to say? Will we blame our lack of action on our favorite television shows, our busy school and sports schedules, or our ignorance? What will be our excuse for our inability to act? I pray you do not live in deception, thinking that God's silence means that He condones or approves of sin. Do not be deceived. God is not mocked. Whatever a man sows, that is what he will reap. If you sow corruption, you will reap corruption. Make no doubt about it. Don't get so friendly with a tolerant Jesus that you have conjured up in your mind that you lose your fearful reverence for Him.

Here is the question of the hour. Where are we going?

There is a significant problem that exists with men all around the world. They do not know where they are going. When a man does not have a destination, he has already arrived at it. He can be comfortably lazy because he has nowhere to go. He has nothing to do. He has no place to be. A man with no destination will try to take any route he desires. Any route looks better than where he sits. It does not matter how perverse or unlawful the route could be. The man will take it if it gives off the appearance of something different. This is why so many men are chasing get-rich-quick schemes and part-time hustles. These routes give a supposed "promise" of wealth or happiness, but oftentimes, they lead the man to hard times, financial difficulty, loss of influence, or jail time.

I firmly believe that if more men put more thought into their future than the clothes they wear, we would have a much better society. I understand that statement stands alone in itself because it is hypothetical by nature. Nonetheless, I want to stress the importance of understanding purpose and progress. We have many men who are moving, but very few of them are actually moving forward.

I know that it can be easy to feel pressured to live up to the expectations of others, or even to define yourself by what you do. You're not who your parents want you to be, you're not who your teachers want you to be, you're not who Instagram wants you to be, and you're not who your friends want you to be. You're not a football player, you're not a math nerd and you're not a trombone player. I remind you, brother, that you are not defined by those things—you're defined by Christ. In Him, you live and move and have your being. Remember this. I want to take this opportunity to teach you some practical steps toward finding your purpose and direction in life, even at a young age:

In order to decide on where you're headed in life, you must first decide that you're going *somewhere*. Make the decision *now* that you will not stagnate, but you will instead move. You will continue to grow. This is the first step. Next, you must recognize that nothing else matters more than bringing glory to God. As yourself this: *What do I enjoy doing that glorifies God?* Think about where your time would be valuably spent. Consider your gifts and talents, and find ways to use them in such way that God is glorified. This may not be an answer that is easily found; this is okay. If you must spend time considering this thought, do so. It is one of the most important questions that you will ever ask yourself.

Rick Warren, in his book *The Purpose Driven Life*, offers an insightful view into finding your purpose. This is the example that he uses: Imagine that you're handed a brand-new invention. You've never seen this item before, so you do not know how to use it. So instead of using the item to fulfill its intended purpose, it sits idly. How must you discover the invention's purpose? You must ask the inventor. The inventor has carefully crafted each intricate detail of his invention. He knows exactly what he has placed within his invention to make it function.

This principal operates in the same way with each and every one of us. Instead of looking toward creation to define you, look to the Creator. Instead of looking to the media to define you, brother, look to God. Ask Him what He has placed inside of you. The Scriptures tell us in Jeremiah 1:5 that God knew you before you were in your mother's womb. He fashioned you for a purpose! In order to discover this purpose, you must inquire of the one who purposed you. As you ponder your purpose, ask the Lord who He has created you to be. Do not be discouraged if it seems as if He does not answer immediately. God does not operate as we do. He may reveal this to you immediately, or He may reveal this to you over time. Whichever it may be, seek Him and trust that He will answer you.

When you realize your purpose and you understand where you're headed in life, then it is time for you to set goals, and to set them accordingly. Do not set meaningless goals for meaningless things. Set goals that will make a lasting, eternal impact. Consider what God has fashioned you to do, and think of reasonable, yet challenging, milestones that you can achieve over time. These are the types of goals that you must set. Consistently refer back to your goals and set new goals frequently. If you must set goals every quarter of the year, then do so. Do what you must to remain disciplined, focused and eternally-motivated.

"ROCKING CHAIR SYNDROME"

Are you familiar with the old-fashioned rocking chair? I know I am. I loved sitting in them when I was younger, and I enjoy them even more now that I am older. My wife says I am an "old-soul." I enjoy rocking in my rocking chair outside, watching people, and sipping a hot cup of tea. That is a good time for me. There are many things I love about the rocking chair, but one sticks out the most. The rocking chair allows me to move without me actually going anywhere. I give myself the feeling of movement, but I do not actually move beyond the spot I first began. I just go back and forth, back and forth, back and forth. Sadly, this is how most men live their lives. They are giving off the appearance of movement, but they are not actually going anywhere. They continue to try doing different things, but nothing seems to work. This is the guy who has a new business every time you see him. He has a new venture every time you talk to him. He has something new he is building, writing, studying, etc. He would not know consistency if it hit him in the face. He has done all these different things for years, but he has not moved ahead. In many ways, it seems like he continues to move further back. He is in the rocking chair of life. He is constantly moving, but he is going nowhere. The only solution for this man is to get up and get moving. Practically, that means he needs to discover his purpose by looking at the talents God has given him. He must get out of the place of mediocrity and begin to challenge himself to move to the next level of his life. Anything that stays still too long is either dead or dying. He cannot afford to stand still. He must get moving.

PASSION AND PURPOSE

What is driving you? Is it ignorance, fear, purpose, etc.?

Purpose is the reason why something is done or created. It is the reason why something exists. When we fail to understand the purpose of something, we eventually abuse it. In that same understanding, when we fail to become knowledgeable about the purpose of something, we allow ourselves to be led by ignorance. Ignorance is the lack of knowledge or information. An ignorant man is one who simply lacks knowledge. A knowledgeable man is one who has knowledge. The main variable in the equation is knowledge, and we know that people fail for their lack of knowledge. The problems that exist in our society today are birthed because of our ignorance. The destruction of our families is born out of our ignorance. We fail for two primary reasons: First, we fail because of what we do not know. Secondly, we fail because we know, but we choose not to follow what we know. That is called rebellion. Let me ask you this question, sir: Are you ignorant, or are you rebellious? Has laziness caused you to ignore the importance of seeking knowledge? Or, has rebellion caused you the to ignore the importance of obedience?

I want you to understand the importance of seeking knowledge especially in the sense of seeking the purpose of why things exist. I want to give you a scenario to consider. At the time of writing this book, I have a beautiful 3-year-old niece who is going on 30. I am trying to prove that she has been on this earth before. Nonetheless, I know that she is a child, and she needs constant supervision. I would be a negligent uncle if I handed her a butcher's knife to go in her room and play with as if it was a doll. I would be a negligent uncle because I should "know" that the butcher's knife is not a toy. The purpose of the knife is to cut. Therefore, the only purpose it could serve in a child's hand is to cut. Since I understand the purpose of the knife, I would not dare put it in the hands of a child. That is irresponsible. However, we do this very thing every single day. Well, we do not give 3-year-olds butcher's knives, hopefully, but we do ignore the purpose of a thing and use it how we see fit. We ignore the purpose of marriage, so it is abused. We ignore the purpose of sex, so it is abused. We ignore the purpose of friends, so they are abused. We ignore the purpose of family, so they are abused. Do you see my point now? We must seek the purpose for everything we set out to do. If we do not, then we are allowing ourselves to be led by ignorance.

And, only an ignorant man enjoys ignorance as his leader. A wise man seeks knowledge.

Let me ask you a couple of questions. I really want you to ponder them. If possible, take some time and write the answers down. Take them to your church group or to your friends and discuss them. What is important is that you think about these questions and really consider the answers.

1. Why are you alive?
2. If you are dating, why are you dating?
3. Why are you involved in that sport or activity?
4. What is the goal you are trying to fulfill before leaving this earth?
5. Who are you serving, and why?
6. Who taught you about life, and was s/he/it a righteous and credible source?
7. What is your greatest frustration, and what brings you the most pain?
8. What are you refusing to deal with in your life right now?
9. If you could do this one thing before you die, what would it be?
10. Do you really know God?

I know you are probably saying, "Cornelius, those questions are all over the place!" You know what? Yes, they are all over the place, but I did that for a purpose. I want to stimulate your mind, and get these kind of questions answered. You may not realize it, but you could have gone 30 years of your life and never answered any of these crucial questions. See, if you have never sat down to ask yourself what is the goal you are after, then how will you ever know if you reach it? If you do not know who you are serving then how will you know how to serve? If you do not really know God then how can you actually say that you are His servant and His follower? How can you say you are called by His voice if you are totally unaware of His voice because you have never heard it? I want and need you to think, brother. I need you to go beyond the normal, ground-level stuff you encounter daily. I need you to embark on a journey to uncover the things that really matter about your life.

There was a story I heard some years ago that I think goes perfectly with this particular chapter. There was an old pilot piloting a plane from Seattle to Alaska. He got on his intercom, and said, "Good evening, ladies and gentlemen! I have some good news, and I have some bad news. The good news is we have a strong tailwind, so we are making excellent time. The bad news is that our navigation system went out on us about an hour ago, so we have no idea where we are right now!" I do not know about you, but I would begin sweating bullets if I heard that come over the intercom. I would be so upset, and I would probably be in my seat asking the Lord to give me patience and peace. Why would I be angry? I would be angry because I *fully expect* for the pilot to *know* where he is headed. He should know the destination. That would be my expectation. Now, make sure you understand me. Isn't it odd that I would *fully expect* for the pilot to know the destination and have directions, but I do not? The flight could last for a couple of hours. I could last without directions for a couple of hours, but I know men who are willing to go their entire lives without directions. I am not sure if that is pride, foolishness, or a mixture of both.

I know there will be some who say, "Well, no one really knows their destination in life." Honestly, I agree with them. However, that does not mean we should not have a general idea of where we are going. As a Christian, I know I plan to delight in Heaven as my eternal home. That is my destination. There is a narrow way to get there, and I must know that narrow path or risk venturing over onto the wide one that leads to destruction.

As believers, our directions are not to "live and learn." Our directions are to "learn and live." God has revealed truths about life. The Bible is our guidebook—a blueprint for living. The Bible gives us meaning, clarity, and fulfillment that cannot be obtained from the world. We must navigate through the wisdom that is contained in the Word of God. We must not allow laziness or rebellion to stop us from doing so.

Personally, I know how it feels to not know your purpose, and I know the feeling of how it is to try to avoid your purpose altogether. I have always been very ambitious. I wanted to run for mayor when I was 17, but the restrictions stopped me from doing it. After I turned 21, I decided to start a campaign for a state representative seat in Georgia. I registered, got the campaign team together, and began what became a very interesting political career. However, the campaign did not last long. Unfortunately, I had a major problem. I only lived in my house for 11 months—not 12. I reached out to some party officials, and they told me not to worry about it. However, my integrity would not allow me to let it go, so I ended the campaign immediately. It was a tough decision to make, but it had to be made. Then, I decided to run for a local city council seat. I decided to go to a potluck to meet some of my opponents for the city council seat. When I arrived, a gentleman walked up to me, introduced himself, and said, "I have some good news and bad news. The good news is that you won't be taking my seat. The bad news is that you live outside of the city limits." Unfortunately, my campaign never got off the ground. I was so depressed after it. I went home, got in my bed fully clothed, and started to go to sleep. While I was drifting off to sleep, the Lord asked me a question that stung to the core of my being. He said, "If you will not do what I have commanded you to do, then why should I open your eyes in the morning?" I immediately jumped out of my bed, fell on my face, and I repented for my rebellion and disobedience. From that day forth, I made it up in my heart that I was a preacher called by Him to deliver His powerful message of deliverance from sin and hell. Brother, it was like a weight was lifted off my shoulders. I was no longer running from my purpose. I was no longer trying to do my own thing. I was finally firmly fixed in what God wanted me to do.

I want you to consider effective and proven leaders like Noah, Paul the Apostle, etc. An effective leader, like Paul, finds out what he is willing to stand for and against. He has done something very few men are willing to do today—he has found a cause that is worth his entire life. I know very few men who are willing to do that today. Rarely do we find men who know where they are going and are willing to give up their lives to get there. As I stated earlier, my ultimate destination is eternal life with my Father. If I am confronted about my faith on earth, and my life is threatened because of my faith then I will have to die. I have found a cause worth dying for. Let me ask you brother: Have you found a cause worth your life? Are you willing to lay everything you have down right now for the cause you say you are championing? Or, are you just living day-to-day with hopes that something will fall out of the sky for you? Noah was a preacher of righteousness who found a purpose worth following. These men identified their purpose and pursued it with passion. What are you following? Is it a GPA? Is it popularity? Is it a girl? Those things are not worth following. They are not worth your life. Do you want to find a cause worth following? If so, begin to study the gospel of Jesus Christ. Ask the Father to allow you to feel His heart towards others. Ask Him to allow you to feel as He feels, see has he sees, and hear as he hears.

As for me, I am devoting myself to knowing my Savior, Jesus Christ. That is my purpose, and Christ is my passion. Preaching is an effect of my passion. Writing books is an effect of my passion. Feeding, giving, lending and serving are all effects of my passion. My ultimate passion is to know my Savior, Jesus Christ, and to share Him everywhere my feet tread. With this purpose, I plan to shape all I do and influence all I lead. Brother, what is your purpose? Is it worth dying for? And, where are you going?

I would be wrong to end this chapter without giving you some practical ways to live with purpose and passion. Understand that every man of faith written about in Scripture was given an assignment that was much larger than himself. The assignment called for sacrifice, commitment, and faith. These are essential to your life as well. Consider Abraham. He was told to leave his father's house, his family, and the land he called home. Then, he was told that he would have a son, but his age caused him to doubt if that would ever come to pass. After having a son, he was told to sacrifice him. All of these things called for sacrifice, commitment, and faith. In the end, Abraham was obedient in leaving, he had his son, and he did not have to kill him.

Consider David. David was a boy who set out to fight a giant Philistine warrior. All David had was his faith in God, and that faith led him to victory. David made some mistakes, and we will cover those in a later chapter. But, in total, David was a man of faith. In fact, it is recorded that he was a man after God's heart. David was a man of sacrifice, commitment, and faith.

I could say the same thing about Moses. He was given a difficult task to lead God's people out of the grasp of a tyrannical dictator to the Promised Land. Unfortunately, Moses did not get there, but it was because of his faith in God that he got anywhere.

I want you to take a moment and read Hebrews 11:1-13. Look at the things these people of faith were able to accomplish because of their faith in God.

Above all things, I want you to realize that success in your life is not dependent on the things you have on earth. For believers, success is defined by obedience to God.

Here are some things I want you to consider doing to help you move forward in your life. I want you to take them as serious as I am right now.

1. **Turn off your television.** You must realize that television is designed to "tell-a-vision." They are telling you their vision for you—not God's. Billions of dollars are pumped into

television every year to increase viewership. They do not care about your emotional, financial, or spiritual health. Their bottom line is increasing theirs. The television has captured more of your time and energy than what you could probably count today. It has stolen some of the most precious, intimate moments that could have given to something productive and beneficial to your eternal health. Instead, you were watching cartoon characters curse at one another, insult their children, and make dirty jokes. Leonard Ravenhill said, "Entertainment is the devil's substitute for true joy." Sir, we must find joy in God before going to search for it in everything else. Turn off your television.

2. **Renew your mind**. Romans 12:2 clearly says "And be not conformed to this world: but be ye transformed by the renewing of your mind, that ye may prove that is that good, and acceptable, and perfect, will of God." This is a simple one. You must renew your mind to the Word of God. I want you ask yourself who has taught you what you know. If the answer is not found in Scripture, then I want you to reevaluate it. You must renew your mind.

3. **Stop procrastinating**. Procrastination is a form of pride. It says, "I am able to put this off until later because I control my time—not God." If God has given you a task to fulfill, you need to fulfill it immediately. Remember that success is about obedience. When God speaks, obey immediately.

4. **Pray**. You must have an ongoing communication with the Father. You must

become vulnerable in prayer to the point where you cry out to Him throughout your day. There is no substitute for prayer. You must pray, and you must pray continuously. It is prayer that God reveals Himself to you. He searches the world looking for a man who is patiently seeking Him. Are you that man? Stop coming up with ideas of flesh to gain some kind of notoriety on earth. Instead, wait until God speaks clearly to your heart the same way He spoke to Nehemiah. Nehemiah was in anguish after seeing the ruined city. He wasn't a preacher. He was a cupbearer for the king. Nehemiah was broken over what he saw, and that sparked passion and purpose in him. What have you begun to chase in this world that was not born out of passion, vulnerability and concern during prayer? If it is not born of our prayer, it is carnal, and it has no eternal value. Those are strong words, and I believe every one of them.

5. **Take responsibility**. Responsibility is an attribute of maturity. In fact, one of the most important aspects of maturity is the willingness to be responsible for yourself and whatever, or whomever, God has placed in your care. The responsibility to cultivate is one of man's greatest objectives. The Garden of Eden was the first place man was called to cultivate, and this directive has traveled from generation to generation until it has touched you and your home. Your personal garden has spread to include your family, your community, and your local

church. Now, you have a responsibility of cultivating that which God has given you and the area where He has placed you. Why else would God send you to a place that's underdeveloped and imperfect? He called you to cultivate it! Be responsible for yourself and what's around you.

A MAN MOST MISERABLE

A man sits alone in his room totally dejected from reality. Temptation knocks at the door of his heart. He has heard that knock time and time again. He is familiar with the consequences that come with allowing temptation to enter his heart, but he shrugs it off. He desires intimacy, attention, and passion, but he doesn't want it from God. He doesn't have enough patience or strength to endure, so he buckles under the temptation of what lies before him. The door swings open, and sin rushes in to overcome and enslave him. He begins to pursue the imitation of what he desires. In what he thinks is private and secret, he eats the trash that's placed before him.

These nightly encounters allow him to feel like a man without ever requiring a thing of him. The images he lusts after and salivates over are fake and unfulfilling; yet, he chooses to be enslaved by them.

He thinks he's a man, but he's not. He's a boy crying out for attention. He's a coward searching for courage in the private chambers of his room, on his phone, and in his head. His devotion isn't real. His words aren't convicting. His faith isn't sure. And, soon enough, his private actions will show in his public performance, and his intellect and submission to temptation will ruin him. He is a man possessed with sin, and sorrow will soon dwell in his house.

Even in your youth, you are responsible for your own decisions. Every decision that you make as you approach maturation in age will determine the caliber of man that you will be. Maturity is much less about age and much more about obedience. Your decision to be obedient now will positively affect everything and everyone that the Lord has entrusted to you in the future. First Timothy 4:12 says, "Let no one look down on [you because of] your youth, but be an example *and* set a pattern for the believers in speech, in conduct, in love, in faith, and in [moral] purity." This scripture is important to remember in your youth. You are responsible to set the standard. You are responsible to lead. You are responsible to grow. I've known 40-year-old men who have the maturity of a child; there are also many 18-year-old men with wisdom and maturity far beyond their years. They are true sons of God, because they begin to emulate Christ through their continuous pattern of obedience. Rather than waiting on age to determine their manhood, they take responsibility for their own actions and decide to grow up mentally, spiritually, and emotionally.

I'm sure that you've experienced, or at least gotten close to experiencing, the danger of pornography. Sitting in what you think are the private chambers of your room, you begin to dive into the possibilities of whatever lust you desire to consume you. With the expansion of technology, your world is open to whatever perversion peaks your curiosity.

You recognize that the images on the screen or in the magazines are fake; yet, they provide you with a visual of your lustful fantasy. They allow you to envision the world you desire to indulge in. The images don't nag, get overly-emotional, complain, or fight back. They stop when you want them to stop. They play when you want them to play. They can far as far as you desire for them to go. The image doesn't require anything of you, except your full attention. Soon or later you become addicted to them. Your hands cannot stop wandering to your crotch. Your eyes cannot stop gazing at the images placed before you. You cannot stop thinking about the images. They consume your day. They consume your years. They consume your life. As time continues, the temptation intensifies.

At times you feel very sorry for you actions, but, even in your times of weaknesses, it's not enough to cause any true repentance. You scream at the top of your lungs, "I LOVE GOD!" but you continue to idolize the images put before you. You continue to allow temptation to eat away at you. You continue to sin to dwell in your heart. You are a man most miserable.

Temptation may lead you to drugs, alcohol, wild partying, or sexual acts outside of marriage. It will consume so much of you that you don't know your right from your left. You will cease from being who you know you can be. You will transform into a man overcome with temptation, and the pressure from it will cause you to become frustrated. You will want what, or who, you know you can't have. The desire will grow into perversion, and you will ride along on a journey where you fail to realize that lust cannot be satisfied. You started out on the journey with a simple curiosity about sex. Now, you're consumed with thoughts of sexual bondage, verbally-abusive sexual escapades, thoughts of homosexuality, cartoon sex, and many other vulgar, perverse thoughts. To ease the frustration, you combine the already consuming fire of temptation and lust with drugs, alcohol, partying, sexual music, etc. The music elevates the temptation. The drugs heighten and loosen you from all constraints. The alcohol removes the boundaries from your standards. Your guard is let down, your standards have all but faded away, and you have become a monster consumed with lust. You are a man most miserable.

You look at masturbation today, and many find ways to justify it. They fail to realize that it's a self-gratifying act of improper reverence to discipline or control. The roots of it are found in the flesh, and pride is the driving slave master. It is carnal in nature, and it lacks any thought for others, even God. The only thought that is given to others concerning masturbation is when it's focusing on taking the intimacy from them so you can satisfy your flesh. It is idolatry at its finest.

Many believe they cannot break free from addictions, such as, masturbation, drinking, smoking, watching pornography, etc. They lack discipline. Condemnation and guilt eats away at them unless their heart is not hardened to the truth. If there is any truth in them, they will be convicted of their wrongdoing. The Holy Spirit will continue to convict them of their wrongdoing, and urge them to righteousness. Unfortunately, many turn their backs to the urging of the Holy Spirit. They spit in God's face and continue their sinful actions. They are men controlled by compulsive habits, and these lustful habits slowly lure them away from God. They harden their hearts and that opens them up for more and more sin. Soon enough, insecurity and inferiority will set in. You will begin to cheapen the act of sex to nothing more than a fleshy rendezvous at your convenience. It doesn't become about satisfying your spouse in marriage or abstaining to honor God outside of marriage. Soon enough, the object of your lustful affection will be nothing more to you but an object—not a true depiction of God's beauty.

Sir, there are many reasons as to why you should resist. Initially, you should fear God. The fear of God is likened to the respect that a son has for his father. In an ideal situation, a father would raise his son in such a way that the son would be afraid to displease him. More than a son fears consequences and more than he fears punishment, he fears letting his father down. This is the same kind of respect that you must have towards God. This is called the fear of the Lord. This may be a foreign concept to you; Maybe your father isn't around, or maybe you don't quite respect him. You may have not had the best example of an earthly father, but your Heavenly Father loves you and disciplines you in a way that is perfect. He will never leave you nor forsake you. He is a good father, worthy of the highest respect. It is the fear of God that keeps men from sinning. And, could it be that you continue to run towards lust because you do not fear God? You may fear man or fear being found out, but you don't fear God. Isn't it something that you fear those things, and people, but you do not fear God, the one who can cast both your body and soul in hell? I ask that you take a vey close analysis of your life. Do you really love God? If you did, you would obey Him. Do you really want to break out of your miserable bondage of lust, drugs, alcohol, or whatever consumes you? Do you really want to end the habit that has plagued your life for years? Do you really want to continue living the way you've been living? ANSWER THOSE QUESTIONS! Sir, are you nothing more than a liar and a hypocrite? Are you nothing more than a self-imposed shell of a boy longing for attention? Are you truly a follower of Christ, or are you just another little boy parading around as if his life is okay?

Break free from those chains of bondage. Have you not heard that Christ came so that you may be set free? And, if He has set you free, then why do you continue to live in bondage? The jail doors have been opened, the handcuffs have come off, and the way has been paved for you to walk freely; yet, you sit there in that lowly cell where sin eats away at you. Jesus Christ is the key that opens the door, but you refuse Him! Sir, why do you refuse the only answer to your freedom? Why do you continue to live in darkness while proclaiming the light? You are a liar, an unrepentant soul, and a man most miserable.

I urge you to repent. That means that you turn from the sin that once held you bondage. Cry out to God that He would break that chain of sin that binds you. Resist the urge and the temptation that arouses your body and mind to sin. Don't tell me that you're resisting and fighting, because I know you're not! Resisting doesn't end until the resistance has lost its power against you. Resistance doesn't stop and admit defeat; therefore, resist! Fighting doesn't mean lying down and allowing yourself to be defeated. It means holding up your sword, bearing your shield, and continuing to fight even when you're tired. Don't you know that in your weakness, God is your strength? Before telling me that you've resisted the temptation, I want you to consider if you've ever resisted temptation to the point of shedding blood. If you have yet to resist to the point of shedding blood, then, sir, you haven't resisted sin.

You must repent, and you must renew your mind. Stop watching those television shows that eat away at your mind and steer your mind from Christ. Resubmit your sexual organs to God, and submit your sexuality to Him as well, if that is your current struggle. Don't try to search for soothing words or verses you could twist to justify your sin. Instead, submit your entire mind, body, will, and emotions to God. Resist all the urges that come up. Turn off the radio, and talk with God instead. Focus on what is pure, excellent, and holy. Ask God to lead you to a brother who can hold you accountable. Uncover what's hidden in your life. Bring it all out in the open. Let the light shine brightly on your darkness and your secrets. Confide in your brother(s) so you will have accountability. Don't be ashamed of your past. Simply put, everyone has a past. Just understand that you desire freedom from what torments and haunts you. There is a way to escape your misery, and Jesus is that way!

GOD'S MAN

We live in a society where knowledge is crowned king. While I believe in knowledge, I'm quick to tell even the seasoned of men that knowledge alone is dead. For the believing man, his knowledge must be coupled with power if he expects to make any lasting changes in his life, his family, and his community.

Many men run to do good things. They strive, stretch, and strain to be good actors who perform great actions, but they lack one thing—prayer. Notice that none of the disciples asked Jesus to teach them how to preach. They asked Him to teach them how to pray. It's in prayer that men receive power. It is in prayer that sermons come alive. It's in prayer that lives are changed even when words aren't spoken. It's in prayer that communities are transformed. It's in prayer that strongholds are broken. It's all found in prayer.

Sir, I'm not sure what post you will try to maintain in your journey to manhood, but I would like to caution you—no matter what assignment you may be given. I want to caution you to pray. Don't seek a pulpit. The power isn't in the pulpit. The power is in the man, but God must first transform the man. He must do such a work in him that he hates the sin he once loved. He must do such a work in him that his life is a reflection of holiness. If the man still goes to preach without carrying the banner of holiness, he will stand before men void of power and lacking great depth. Even the smartest of men will fail in providing any lasting truth, even those who do nothing more than stand and recite verse upon verse upon verse of the Bible. See, the words on the page mean nothing if the man who speaks them has nothing. This isn't to devalue what's written in the Bible. What I'm writing here furthers the point that the words written are inspired by our holy God; therefore, men, who carry those same holy standards, must preach them. If the man chooses not to preach them, he still isn't able to neglect the responsibility of pursuing holiness in all things.

Sir, your life must be given over to pure worship. You must go before God with no motives of your own. You must release all your plans, ideas, and schemes. He will not compete with you. It is His plan to transform you so you are fully equipped to carry the rugged cross. Notice that God sent a man to prepare the way for His Son, Jesus Christ. That man was John the Baptist. John was a man of passion. God sent His only Son in the form of man to die for our sins. Even Jesus portrays the significance of prayer. He was always about the Father's business, and we know He knew the Father's business because He knew the Father. He wasn't about the priests business in the synagogue. He wasn't thinking of new plans or new ministries to build to further the truth. He submerged himself in prayer. He is dipped down in anguish. He is fully drenched in holiness. He isn't a man's man. Oh, no! He's God's Man. We notice in the ministry of Peter that power didn't come because he was knowledgeable. Peter was a fisherman. It was Paul that was skilled in knowledge.

Peter was worker. It was Paul that was an intellect. Yet, God sent Peter, and the other disciples, to the Upper Room so they may pray and be intimate with Him (Acts 1:12-28). Once Peter emerges, He is dripping in the Holy Spirit's presence. He is fully engulfed in God's passion. He goes in a man's man, but he comes out God's man. In Acts 2, you notice his fiery sermon. After Peter preaches, the people are pierced to their hearts because of what they heard. They had nothing else to ask but what are they to do after hearing such powerful preaching. Pay attention to what I'm about to say: Many will think that it was Peter's sermon that captivated the hearts of those who were listening. No! It wasn't the sermon. Any man could've said those words. What captivated the hearts of those men and women was the passion that dripped from each word. The people felt the conviction because the words originated from a convicted man. They were pierced in their heart because God first pierced Peter's heart while he was in the Upper Room.

God is not in search of better methods. He doesn't need your ways of being more productive. His plan is simple—He desires to break and mold men into His men. Everyone today is looking for a better method, but God is looking to transform a few good men. Will you be one of those men? Will you relinquish your own will so that God may work through you, or will you settle for being just a man's man? What will become of you in eternity? What will the Lamb's Book of Life record of you? Will it be that you did great things, oversaw great organizations, or acted in great performances? Or, will it be that you stood before God, fully ready for Him to mold you in His image and His likeness? What will you do?

This is your moment of truth. If you choose to ignore it, I pray that God has mercy on your soul. I'd also ask that you relinquish the title of a Christian, because your following is in vain. If you won't follow Him wholeheartedly, then consider that you're not following Him at all.

Our society doesn't need more little boys trying to operate in a godly man's arena. Our society doesn't need more actors. It doesn't need more men trying to perform great works. What it needs is more men who are committed to prayer. We need men who are willing to allow the Holy Ghost to flow through them. We need men who will labor to be anointed by God in the intimacy of prayer. It is only in those times of intimacy that God will empower the lifeless soul of man. Sir, I ask that you go to get life. Yearn for it. Cry out for it. And, realize that this life far exceeds the shallowness of what many have come to know as following Christ today. Notice that Christ commands his disciples to come and follow Him. These men gave up their lives for the Gospel. They gave up their careers. They gave up their identity. They left it all. I beg of you, do not be afraid to abandon the presence of earthly kings; you will one day spend eternity with the King of Kings and Lord of Lords. Your small sacrifice of a life today will mean everything in eternity.

Don't consider this as a light thing because, sir, it is not. It is God who makes, conforms, and transforms you. It is God who makes the preacher. It is the preacher who preaches the Gospel, both with and without words, to his family and his community. The sermon is not the more important part of the preacher, and, yes, there is a preacher in all of us men. I don't know what pulpit you'll stand behind, even if it's unconventional; but I do know you will preach—whether with or without words. The sermon you both preach and live isn't made in a couple of hours of studying. The sermon, which is the culmination of your life and God's special endowment of wisdom, is born over time. As the life within you matures, the sermon you both live and preach matures. Do you see the correlation here? The voice is lifeless if the Holy Spirit has yet to fill you. If you are puffed up with knowledge, then your words, even when used correctly, will have no life in them. You will be like a trumpet blowing with no air. You can scream, but no words will come out. You can sweat, but no words will convict. You can make the audience dance, but no power will originate from your preaching, neither verbal nor nonverbal, because you are void of power.

Don't be another dead man preaching dead sermons. Don't be another man living dead sermons, either. Simply put, men devoid of power are dead. Dead men both preach and live dead sermons, and dead sermons kill. They don't bring life because there is no life in them.

Sir, everything depends on your intimacy with God. Everything depends on your surrendering to God. You must become impregnated with passion. You must go before other men fully-clothed in humility. In other words, there must be no pride found in you. There is no job that is below you to accomplish or fulfill at our Master's request. You must be fully mendable and ready to go at His request—even if it angers or saddens those around you. You must be harmless as a dove, wise as a serpent, and have the faith of a child. This journey of manhood you are on will take everything in you to accomplish, but you must see it through. It will have to be heroic, compassionate, faithful, courageous, and fearless. Timid men will not last. Men who thrive on the praises of people will die once they criticize them. Men who desire to please others will soon grow tired and abandon all he does. If the man is weak in faith, he won't be able to hold on to God or His Word.

You, sir, must follow in the steps of godly men who have walked before us. You must not be a man's man. You must be God's man, and God shapes His men in prayer. God's man is formed in the closet, not on the stage or behind the pulpit—no matter what pulpit he stands behind. It doesn't matter if the man tries to put on the shoes of men before him. The man won't be successful unless he, too, is baptized in passion through prayer. I beg of you to consider what you have read. Don't turn this page without falling to your face to ask God to reveal to you what you have just read. This is not a joke. It is not a game. You want to be a man? If so, humble yourself and pray. Turn from your sins, and pursue righteousness. Die to all the ills of the enemy, and come alive to all that is born of God. Resist temptation. Flee sexual immorality. Be awakened to God, and become immersed in His presence. You will find joy there. You will find refuge there. You will find power there.

THE MAN OF GOD

We are obsessed in our society with the thought of being a "man of God." It has become a common phrase in the Christianese language. Many have become accustomed to using such language when describing men they know who are in active participants in the church body. Nevertheless, have you ever asked yourself what it means to be a man of God? For example, we have the pastor who is charged to lead and be an example to the Shepherd's flock. But, does the man of God only rest with the pastor, the evangelist, the prophet, the teacher, or the apostle?

1 Samuel 9:5-8 reads, "When they came to the land of Zuph, Saul said to his servant who was with him, 'Come, and let us return, lest my father cease to be concerned about the donkeys and become anxious for us.' And he said to him, 'Behold now, there is a man of God in this city, and the man is held in honor; all that he says surely comes true. Now let us go there, perhaps he can tell us about our journey on which we have set out.' Then Saul said to his servant, 'But behold, if we go, what shall we bring the man? For the bread is gone from our sack and there is no present to bring to the man of God. What do we have?' And the servant answered Saul again and said, 'Behold, I have in my hand a fourth of a shekel of silver; I will give it to the man of

God and he will tell us our way.'" We must notice that Saul knew of this man because he was an honorable man. This means that he was esteemed or held in high estimation because of his words and his actions. To be referred as the man of God would mean that he was given a very honorable title that did not fit for every man in the city. It means something of value and prestige.

The 'man of God' title is not one that is bestowed on a man just because he claims to walk with God. Instead, the 'man of God' title is one that is earned over time because of his words and his actions. His words and his actions prove that he truly is a man of God. If the man's testimony doesn't reflect that of honorable words and actions then, it is safe to conclude that he is not a true man of God. If the man doesn't bear fruit of the Father, then how can we possibly assume that the man is truly a man of God? We would be liars to say that a adulterer and a thief were men of God; yet, we use that title so loosely. Nowadays, any man that claims God as his father is considered a man of God, even if his life doesn't show fruit of the honor that is due to the title he proclaims.

Our problem is that most pulpits are filled with men who think or want to be considered men of God. However, their private lifestyle doesn't match their public affirmation. They claim to be one person in public while committing spiritual-adultery in private. The man of God should be far away from all lies. He should not promise one thing but do another. He should be upright in his actions and clear in his approach. He should be direct and straightforward. He should be work with integrity and class. If he says he's going to pay something, he should pay it. If he says he is going to do something, he should do it. His private words and his deeds should match his public words and deeds. Don't be deceived. The production of godly character isn't produced behind a pulpit in front of scores of people; it's produced in private. You can't proclaim one thing then live another way. That is the epitome of living a lie; the man of God doesn't live a lie.

I have been both the liar and the one who was lied to. I know what it's like to promise someone I'd help them only to not respond or help them when they were in need. I've repented of such action. However, I use it to say that I have recognized it as wrong, and you should recognize it as well. Don't wimp out on your commitment. Honor your commitment. If you told a missionary you would help him or her, do it. When you see trash in your neighbor's yard, go pick it up. It may not be your trash, but it is in your community. Earn the title that you want to proclaim, and don't steer away from the responsibility. I want to mention a few things that I truly believe are characteristics of the man of God.

RESPONSIBLE

Who can find a responsible man nowadays? Are you responsible? Do you take care of your responsibilities? Are you passionately pursuing the call that God has given you for your life, or are you okay with not taking the responsibility?

Here's the thing you may not realize: When you do not take responsibility for your life, you are ultimately making someone else take responsibility for it. You are giving someone else a heavier load because you refuse to carry your own. As a pastor, I hear the most heart-wrenching stories. Most times, they have to deal with marriage and the children. Most times, the husband has mentally checked-out of the marriage, and the he no longer cares about the children. He is present in the house, but he is very silent. The man doesn't take on the responsibility of being the spiritual example in the home, so it places more responsibility on the shoulders of the woman. She wakes the kids up early for Sunday morning service, gets them dressed, drives them there, makes sure dinner is going to be ready when she returns, and makes sure everyone is satisfied both at the Sunday assembly and at home. She does all of this while the man wakes up late and prepares for the sport's game to come on television. He uses the excuse that it's his day to rest, but that only means that he has actually given her more work. A man who doesn't take responsibility for his actions and his life is worse than an infidel.

I'll never forget the lessons my mother taught me about responsibility. There were certain times when the trash had to go outside. It was my responsibility to make sure the trash was out of the house and in front of the house for the garbage man to collect it. Failure to do so meant I would have to suffer the consequences. There was one time that I did not do it. I did not take out the garbage, and I was shocked because there were no immediate consequences. The trash sat there in the kitchen for a couple days. Then, one day I heard my mother call my name from downstairs. I raced downstairs to see what was the problem. She pointed towards the trash can, and all I could see were ants crawling all over it. I knew that she was not pleased, and I knew that I was going to pay for it. I had to take out the trash, which was covered in ants, and I had to clean up all the ants that got into the house. It took me almost 3 hours to finish everything. Looking back, I finally realized what my mother taught me. I could have spent 15 minutes taking out the trash, which was my responsibility, instead of spending 3 hours taking out trash and cleaning up a huge pile of ants. I learned a valuable lesson that day that has stuck with me until now. I cannot afford to be lazy and shrink back on my responsibility. I cannot afford not to teach my family, honor my commitments, and stick firmly to what I have spoken. I have to be responsible, and so do you.

I don't know what your responsibilities are, but I recommend you do not put them off. Don't procrastinate on your chores. Don't make the rest of your household suffer because you're not holding up your end of the bargain. When you graduate and either attend college or start living on your own, you will have to be responsible for the cleanliness of your own home; start practicing now. Get up and help around the house. Don't drag along in school. Don't fall behind on your coursework. Don't waste time at your job. Take initiative. Be an example. Honor your commitments. Be responsible.

LOYAL

Who can find a loyal man nowadays? I don't want you to assume that I'm talking about loyalty in the area of friendships. Instead, I'm talking about loyalty to God. Oftentimes, you hear about the loyalty you are to have with your friends, your family, your teachers and your peers. However, how often do you hear about the loyalty you should have with God? Is He not more important than some kind of carnal loyalty? What good is it to be totally loyal to a friend, but not be loyal to God? If a so-called friend asked you to lie about something, would you do it, or would you decline the offer because you are loyal to God? You realize that He doesn't tolerate lying; therefore, don't lie.

Look at your friendships and your different associations. Do they have more of your attention than God? Do you depend on their words more than God's? If a so-called friend told you to do something dishonorable, would you do it even if it means that you destroy your good name and character?

Don't be deceived. Loyalty to humans is fickle. Most times, it is based on feelings, and, sadly enough, feelings change. Once the feelings change, the friendship changes. When they see that you no longer want to go to the club, they don't like you anymore. They notice that you talk differently, think differently, and act differently, and they don't like it. Their feelings towards you will change, and the relationship will fade right along with it.

Many times, I get stories about young men who are involved in gangs. They enjoy the family atmosphere and the camaraderie they get from being associated with such thugs. It makes them feel wanted and desired. To be initiated in the gang, the young man will have to undergo a strenuous initiation ritual that could range from committing a horrible crime or enduring a terrible beating. Many times, this doesn't differ from the hazing that takes place in a fraternity. In actuality, a fraternity is nothing more than a legalized gang unit. Nevertheless, the gang, as well as the fraternity, stresses the importance of loyalty. You must know the signs, the codes, the order, the organization, etc. so you are familiar and capable of remaining loyal to them. Unfortunately, you cannot be loyal to both God and those associations. You cannot esteem the words of the fraternal order over the commands of God. You cannot honor the words of your so-called friends over the words of God. God must come first in your life. He must be primary, never secondary. The gangs that initiate these young men require their loyalty, and, unfortunately, they give it to them. Now, let me ask you: Have you given your loyalty to some organization, whether it's legal or not? Have you given your loyalty to some person, no matter the title she or he possesses in society? Where does your loyalty lie?

See, the man of God is loyal to his wife, his children, and God, and he associates himself with those who are loyal to God. That is what makes the association that of a family unit. When I meet another pastor, I expect to meet a man who is loyal to God. If he isn't loyal to God, I know he won't be loyal to me. When I advise couples concerning their marriage, I always like to get information concerning their lifestyle. I want to have an idea as to if the man is loyal to God. If he isn't loyal to God, it's almost certain that he won't be loyal to his wife. Ultimately, the loyalty we have to God is paramount and shows us the degree of loyalty we will have with one another.

Look at Matthew 12:50. Jesus says, "For whoever does the will of My Father who is in heaven is my brother and sister and mother." Jesus makes a clear distinction of His loyalty and where it lies even in terms of blood relatives. My brothers, or *bro* as many of us like to call each other, are not those who follow the will of the devil. My brothers are those who do the will of my Father in heaven. You're not in this family unit, which is clamped by faith, if you aren't committed to the will of the Father. Ultimately, brother, where does your loyalty lie? Evaluate your life. Makes the necessary changes. Be loyal to our God.

FAITHFUL

Proverbs 20:6 reads, "Most men will proclaim every one his own goodness: but a faithful man who can find?" A faithful man is trustworthy and dependable. When he says he is going to be somewhere, he is there. You don't have to ask any questions about it. If he doesn't show up, you know there was a problem beyond his control. You know he would do anything in his power to be there because you know he is faithful. The faithful man considers his faithfulness to God to be the hallmark of his life. He is proud of it, he proclaims it, and he lives it.

God is faithful. We can trust that He will do just as He promised. We have a promise that all the children of disobedience will be punished for their disobedience. Just because the punishment is not immediate doesn't mean it will not come. In the same way, the man of God is faithful to his promises. When he makes one, he does everything within his power to keep it. If God were not faithful, then we would be in a world of trouble. The faithfulness of God sustains the earthly life we all live. He waters the grass that feeds the livestock, nurtures the soil that creates a breeding ground for worms for the birds, and makes sure the ocean waves come only so far up the shore. Without His faithfulness, we would all be doomed. What about you though? What about your faithfulness in the assembly you attend weekly? When you go to church, are you known as a faithful person there who is willing to walk the streets to minister to the lost, cook food to cater to the hungry, pick up the trash in the parking lot, cut the grass for an ailing congregant, or take some time out to see about a child who is fatherless? Can people depend on you to get the job done, or are you just a hindrance?

I never want to be the person that people know as the one who never does anything. I know you know someone like that, and I pray you're not that person. I have a couple guys in my life who are like that. When I call them, I know not to expect much at all. When they say they're going to be somewhere, I don't count on it. I expect absolutely nothing from them; therefore, I am never disappointed. There was one time that I was supposed to meet one young man for lunch. I sat there waiting for about 15 minutes. Finally, I got a text that said he was on his way. I sat there, and I sat there, and I sat there. I would get call after call saying that he was close. Then, about 2 hours later, I got a call saying that he had to get his oil changed in his car, and he was going to be late. I was heated because I hate when my time is wasted! I can never get those hours back, and I hate I wasted them sitting and waiting on him to arrive. Needless to say, I left the place, and he never arrived. He called me some days later to give me the reason as to why he never showed up. I listened; however, I knew who I was dealing with at that moment. I knew I couldn't trust him to be faithful to his word. Nonetheless, I gave him another shot. We scheduled another outing, and he stood me up again. That was the straw that broke the camel's back. I have no ill-will towards him, simply because I know the kind of man I'm dealing with. He is unfaithful. The day finally came that he asked me if I could help him look for a job. I was terribly torn. I could definitely help him; however, I could not write him a favorable recommendation simply because I know his level of unfaithfulness. As an owner of several companies, I am very always very sensitive to the recommendations I write and receive for potential employees. I want to make sure I do not lie by deceiving the hiring employee. I wouldn't want some unfaithful man working in my company. His unfaithfulness will require someone else to make sure his work got done, and no one wants that to happen.

Understand that faithfulness is very important, and it cannot be ignored. It is truly a fruit of the Spirit. Those who are faithful are following in the traits of God. That is an honorable thing, and it must be shared with all men.

HONORABLE

When you are honorable you are worthy of honor. Honor is simply having integrity. Such integrity will allow you to be distinguished and highly respected. You earn an honorable title; it should not just be given to you. What merit does a title have if it has not been earned? Think about all the titles you use to describe yourself. Have they been earned? Do you really identify yourself in those titles? Are you all caught up in those titles?

I know many men who ask to be referred by their titles. They want you and others to know that they are titled appropriately. Unfortunately for them, I care more about a kitten playing in the middle of a field than I do about some arrogant use of a title. For some reason, they think using that title brings them honor even when they do not deserve it.

One of God's commands is to honor your mother and father. It is the command that comes with a promise of longevity of life. If you honor your parents, you will ultimately live longer. With that being said, you must understand that honoring your parents means that you will not try to ruin their name in the community. You recognize that stealing and lying could potentially harm, if not ruin, their good name so you stay away from it. You do whatever you have to do to make sure they are honored. I always wanted to make sure I wasn't dishonoring my parents name in the community, but even that didn't stop me from doing things that could have ultimately hurt them. I was a thief, a liar, and a whore. Those things could've greatly damaged my parent's good name; however, I did them. They weren't honorable or appropriate to my parents or to God. Ultimately, I didn't truly begin to honor my parents until I began to truly honor God. Then, I finally realized that honoring my parents would result in my truly honoring God.

In 2006, I dropped out of college. It was a very rough time for me because I had no worldly substantial reason for leaving except that God told me to do it. I was challenged on every way by everyone about my decision, but I knew what I heard was true. Years later, I have the proof to show that what I heard was true; however, it was a real struggle back then. As time passed, I was sure that I ruined my family's name and God's name by associating it to my leaving college. However, I stuck with what I heard until finally, the fruit began to show. The people who called me crazy began to want to be around me. They wanted my help. Those who doubted me wanted to work with me. Those who talked about me wanted to talk with me. Things were beginning to change, and, ultimately, God got the glory and the honor out of it. That must be true for your life as well. Make sure God gets the honor out of what you do, and be sure to live your life honorably so you are worth the respect you ask for.

PASSIONATE

To be strongly convinced and emotionally-charged about a person or a thing is to be passionate. Passion is more than a simple word used to describe carnal lust. It is an intense enthusiasm that cannot be underestimated. Oftentimes, we consider the sufferings of Christ between the night of the Last supper and to His death to be a time of great passion. Simply put, passion is an intense suffering cultivated from within.

I want you to evaluate your life. Discover what you're passionate about. What are you emotionally-charged about? Is it a person, an idea, or a thing? Are you passionate about sports, wealth, prestige, power, fashion, women, or intellect? What is that intense suffering that's being cultivated within you, and is it righteous?

I ask you to consider your own passions because I had to consider my own at one time in my life. I had to evaluate my life to see whether or not my passions were just and righteous. Ultimately, I concluded that they weren't. I was once extremely passionate about politics. It ran my life. I tried to run for political office at the age of 17, but I couldn't even enter the race because I wasn't old enough. I tried again; yet, I was still unsuccessful. I would watch CSPAN, a political television network, for hours. I would clear my schedule so I was available to watch every State of the Union address, every inauguration, every speech that was aired, watch every political commercial I could catch, etc. I was fully-immersed and deeply-passionate about political office. Then, my time came to finally run for office. I chose to run for a state seat in Georgia. I started my campaign, and it was off to a great start. However, I had one major problem. I did not fully meet the residency requirement to be elected. I contacted the party leaders to let them know of the error, and someone told me to run anyway. He stated that people did it all the time. At that moment, I was stuck between a decision that would follow me all the days of my life. I could have decided to go through with it knowing I would be risking my future if I was ever found out. I could have done it knowing full-well that I was lying. I could have acted dishonorably and, ultimately, ruined my witness. I did not continue the campaign, even though the passion I had for it was strong. There was something there I didn't really want to admit, but I was left with no other choice once I was given this decision to make. I had to admit to myself that my passions were based in pride and selfishness. I didn't really want to run for the betterment of people; I wanted to do it for myself. I was going to be another politician who was more concerned about himself than the constituents. My passion was clear, but highly prideful and unrighteous.

Are there any areas in your life that you're willing to compromise on because you're passionate about them? You may have given your life to Christ, but recognize that this means that you must also surrender your passions to Him. Are your passions displaced? Are there areas in your life that you give more attention to than Christ? Any passion that competes with Christ must be laid at the foot of the cross. Pray to God to redirect your passions. Ask Him to teach you how to use your passions to glorify Him, rather than glorifying yourself. Learn how to take what you care about most and redirect it towards Christ.

See, the man of God has passions that are singular in purpose. This means that he is passionate about everything that God is passionate about. Peter writes that it is God's desire for all men to be saved and come into the knowledge of the truth. That is God's desire; therefore, that should be the man of God's desire. The man of God should spend his waking hours contemplating the singular passions of God. God is passionate about holiness, and He expects us to live holy, as He is holy. Are you passionate about holiness, or are you consumed with lust, bitterness, and pride? Are your days filled with things that elevate you rather than those things that promote the righteous message of Christ? Think, man, think! What are your passions? Are you so overly-consumed with sports and entertainment that you don't have any room left to focus on those things that are at the center of God's heart? If so, don't dare refer to yourself as a man of God. You're not a man of God; you're a man of flesh and worldly pleasure. You're a man consumed with worldly junk and deadly, venomous cravings.

What are your thoughts when you rise in the morning? What are your thoughts before you go to bed at night? Are you truly focused on what's pure and holy, or are you concentrating on what's on the television? Do you spend more time being taught in worldly intellect than you do being taught in the Word of God? Notice that the man of God is of God! That means that he is passionate and takes on the very nature of God. He is consumed with God's words, and we know that he is only able to consume those words when he takes time to truly feed on them. The man of God's passions are not by chance; they are on purpose. Are yours?

INDUSTRIOUS

I started working when I was 15. In many eastern countries, that is considered old. I don't want to gloat about my working because most of it was dishonest. I worked at a concession stand where I sold stadium food like hotdogs, pretzels, etc. Then, I began selling alcohol to the same stadium patrons. Then, I sold nachos, ice cream, etc. I would work 9 to 10 hours a day. Some days, I worked 21 to 23 hours. I would go to work after school, and still have to make sure my homework was completed. I did it while taking Advanced Placement, or college-level courses, in high school. It was very tough; however, there was no feeling like being able to provide for myself because of my hard work. I was becoming less dependent on my mother and father. I was able to buy my first car with cash. I worked up enough money to pay $550.00 for my 1997 Nissan Mazda Protégé. That car was my prized possession. I drove it like it was top-of-the-line. It meant something to me because I knew I worked hard for it. I kept it clean because it was mine, and I knew the sweat it took to get it. When it was time for me to go to college, I was able to pay for everything that my scholarships didn't cover without my parents having to pay anything. The look on my mother's face was priceless when I told her that I was able to pay for all my books, living expenses, and everything else I needed. At that moment, I felt industrious and proud of the work I had done.

Nowadays, I look around at many of the men in our society, and I see just how lazy they have become. They are not industrious at all. They show up late for work, but they still expect to get paid more for their terrible effort. They expect to get a promotion on their jobs, but they do nothing that earns one. They are not diligent in their assignment. Many of them don't have a clue as to what God told them to do, simply because many of them are too lazy to ask Him. They do not want to labor in prayer for an answer. They want what our society loves to give—quick and instant success without any labor. Look at many of the so-called "men of God" today. They harp on and on and on about God giving them something just because they ask for it. They want it NOW, and they want it BIG! But, they do nothing but complain and remain lazy. If you're one of those men, please allow for me to caution you before you go demanding our holy God for your selfish requests. You had better be glad He doesn't condemn you to an eternal hell, because that is truly what you deserve! However, He sent His only Son to die on the cross for your sins. But that really means nothing to you, huh? If that doesn't stir you up, then it's safe to say that you're flat-lining fast!

Look at the society we have today. What happened to the righteous pride that comes from righteous labor? What happened to hard work and diligence? Where is it? What happened to it? Did the fathers and preachers stop preaching it, teaching it, and portraying it? Is our excuse that you didn't have an example? If so, please let me tell you that it is a very sorry excuse! Jesus is a perfect example of diligence and hard work. He was always about His Father's business. He was diligent in prayer even when His disciples would go to sleep while they were supposed to be praying. His diligence didn't come and die away. In fact, He was diligent from His youth to the cross. When Mary and Joseph went looking for Him, they found Him learning in the temple. He was about His Father's business. At His death, He would not forgo drinking of the cup of wrath because He was still about His Father's business.

Let me ask you, sir. Are you about the Father's business, or are you about your own? Are you industrious like our Savior, Jesus Christ? Even He gave of Himself to work. He was a carpenter, and, most importantly, He was a skilled teacher. He didn't waste time being idle and lazy. He knew His life was for a purpose, and He met that purpose with passion. Are you so consumed with time with the guys, entertainment, chasing women, running after your idea of success, etc. that you have lost focus on true diligence and hard work? Are you working hard for worldly gain without even considering eternity? Ask yourself these questions, and begin to reevaluate your life to see if you are as industrious as our Savior, Jesus Christ.

HUMBLE

Humility has been lost in our day. We live in a society where it's socially correct to exalt man, and his ways, above all things. When you think of the word "humble," I want you to think specifically of the word "submission." Oftentimes, we, as men, do not hear that word unless we are referring to a wife submitting to her husband in marriage. However, submission does not stop there. It doesn't even begin there. Our best example of submission is between Jesus and the Father. Jesus refers to Himself as the way. He says that He is the truth and the light. He also portrays Himself as being the only savior. What He does not do is try to override the will of the Father. He submits in His position as the Son, and He does not try to take the position as the Father. He recognizes that He is only one Person of the Triune God. He doesn't assume all power away from the Spirit and the Father. That is true submission.

Jesus could have had many of his aggressors killed instantly. He could have called down legions of angels to destroy many of those who opposed Him; however, He did not. He remained true to being submissive and humble.

Now, let's look at your life. The man of God is of God; therefore, he takes on the very characteristic of humility. He is submissive in terms of the order of things. He does not try to usurp the authority of his earthly boss. Instead, he does the work he has been assigned to do. He works as unto the Lord instead of trying to work to prove himself to man and flesh. He is not arrogant and overbearing. He doesn't have to have the attention or the spotlight. He is focused on one thing, and that is to be obedient to the will of the Father. This allows him to remain humble in every situation he finds himself. When he's called names, he chooses to take them even though he knows they are not true. When he is slapped on the cheek, he offers the other even though he knows he did nothing wrong. When he is beat, stoned, crucified upside down, etc., he still follows the will of the One who sent him. He remains submitted and humble. He respects authority and the laws that are given. If you still live in your parent's house, then, as a man of God, you should respect the laws of the house. See, the man of God isn't rebellious for rebellion's sake. He is submissive and humble to authority, but he is direct and passionate about speaking the truth—even if it means he will die for it. If authority tells him to bow his knee to another god, he will not do it. If authority tells him to break one of God's commands, he will not honor it. He only honors the commands of God, and he does it at all costs. He is humble and submissive. He is a man of God.

I want you to notice something that is very peculiar about the man of God. See, the man of God ceases from being the man of God if he is not one with God. You may notice that the title of this chapter is "The Man and God" instead of "The Man of God." We cannot assume that we can take on His characteristics without first carrying His seed and likeness. How can we be like Him unless we have been born of Him? Sir, have you been born of God? Do you know Him, or are you only knowledgeable about Him?

I meet countless men who can quote many Scriptures. They have more degrees than a thermometer; however, they lack one essential truth—they do not know God. They do not know Him intimately. They do not have an ongoing learning relationship with Him. They know what others have said about Him, but they do not know Him. They know what others have called him, but they do not know Him. Their knowledge of Him is based on second-hand knowledge, and many are fine with that. However, that cannot be true for you. In order for you to be a man of God, you must first be a man who is born of God.

David was a man of God because He was man after God's own heart. Ezekiel was a man of God because he was with God. Joseph was a man of God because God walked with Him. Noah was a man of God because He stood true to do what He was told, and he was a preacher of righteousness. Do you notice what these men have in common? They were men of God because they were men with God. They did not carry the characteristics without completely carrying His likeness.

I love the Apostle Paul. In a letter to Galatia, he writes "From now on let no one cause trouble for me, for I bear on my body the brand-marks of Jesus" (Galatians 6:17). The Apostle Paul tells them that he is branded. He bears the brand of Jesus Christ. Now, this is a man of God! As a child, I grew up in the country in Newton, Mississippi. It was common for me to see a cow being branded with a hot brander. The cow would bear the initials of the owner so that, if it got lost, it could be returned to its owner. Do you see what Paul is saying here? He's saying that he has the brand mark of Christ! He wears the brand of our Savior! He is marked, and he welcomes whatever comes with that mark—even if it includes death. Are you branded? Are you a true man of God by words and deeds, or are you a man of God by title alone? If you can only call yourself a man of God, then it's safe to assume that your title is just as weak as the foundation it stands on.

THE MAN WITH GOD

You just read an entire chapter devoted to the man of God. However, I would be wrong not to include this chapter in this book, which is purposed to allow you to truly think about your life and your relationship with God.

Let me tell you a story.

A local villager named Thomas was working in the field as the heat from the sun beamed on him. After every pick of the yielding crop, he would wipe the sweat from his brow. After about 3 hours of being in the hot sun, Thomas went over to the watering hole to get a drink of water. He dipped his head in the watering hole, drank many gulps of water, and quickly brought his head out of the water. After many gulps of the cool water, he lifted his head, and he was amazed at what was standing there before him on the other side of the watering hole. There stood a hungry tiger who was waiting for the right time to pounce on Thomas. Quickly, Thomas jumped from the hole and ran as fast as he possibly could through the field until he got to end of the stony cliff. Noticing that the tiger was right behind him, Thomas decided to jump off the cliff. As he descended down, he grabbed a branch that was barely hanging on to the side of the embankment. Overhead, Thomas could hear the sound of the tiger roaring loudly as he held on for life. He knew that if he let go of that branch, he would ultimately die because of the height of the fall. As his arms began to grow tired, Thomas saw a little rat come out of a small hole where the branch was positioned. The rat began to nibble away at the branch. With each bite, Thomas grew more and more afraid. Out of instinct, Thomas yells out, "God, please save me!"

Overhead, Thomas hears the roars from the hungry tiger, he sees the rat chipping away at the branch, and then he hears a voice say to him, "Thomas, do you really want to be saved?" Thomas says back, "Yes, I want to be saved! Please save me!" The voice replies back, "It will take strength and faith." Thomas screams back, "I'll do anything you tell me! Just save me!" The voice calmly says back to Thomas, "Okay. I want you to let go of the branch." Thomas looks up at the hungry tiger and looks ahead at the rat. He lifts his head towards the heavens, and he yells, "Hey! Is anyone else up there? I think I heard the wrong voice!"

I love that story because it has a mixture of so many different elements of man. Consider Thomas in our story, and compare him to your life or the life of other men you may know.

First, Thomas was industrious. He was out in the field working at the sweat of his brow. He wasn't tucked away in some sheltered place. He was out there with all the danger that comes from being outside. When it was time for water, he didn't go grab a bottle. No, he went to retrieve his water from the watering hole where the animals went to drink. Even with the beaming heat from the sun, Thomas lasted 3 hours out in in. He was tough. He was strong. He was hardworking. He was a man.

Secondly, Thomas was alone. There wasn't anyone else out there with him in the field. Even when he hung on that branch, he was alone. Well, he wasn't alone, per se. There were no people around, but God was still with him.

Thirdly, he was conscious of his surroundings. Thomas was able to notice the Tiger was closing in on him. Have you ever been around other men who are unaware of their surroundings? They're just clueless as to what they really need to do, who they could help, or how they could advance something. I know men who can stand in a park that's filled with trash and say, "This park doesn't need anything." They aren't aware of their surroundings. Nonetheless, Thomas was well aware of his.

Lastly, Thomas was a doubter. He believed enough in God that he asked Him for help. I'm sure you believe enough in God to ask Him for help. However, Thomas didn't believe enough in Him to obey Him. His faith wasn't sure. It didn't confidently rest in truth, which, ultimately, comes from God. Thomas, like most men, has a faith built by words but it lacks deeds. It's vast, but it lacks depth. It's externally covered, but internally empty. In fact, it isn't true faith at all. It's just a high expectation based on man's intelligence. Thomas was a doubter, and, although he knew of God, he wasn't quick to follow Him.

I'm not sure if you're that way. I pray you're not, but I'll be honest with you in saying that most men are. They believe there's a God, but very few actually take up their cross to follow Him. They are inconsistent. Their words have no meaning. Their actions are all in vain. Their life is empty. And, their ways are damning.

I don't know what was at the bottom of that fall for Thomas, but I do know that God told him to let go. When Thomas hung on that branch, I'm sure his mind was racing with all kinds of thoughts. He probably thought about dying as soon as he let go. He probably thought about trying to wait the tiger out so he could climb back up, or trying to make the rat stop chewing on the branch. I'm sure he had many thoughts, but none of them stood up to the command from God to let go and fall.

Thomas was there with God, but his lack of faith proved that he wasn't truly the man he thought he was. Instead, he wanted to hear another voice tell him to do something that would seem easy and sensible. He wanted to hear something that wouldn't require him to have faith, but we, as men, should know that we only please God by faith. Truth is known by obedience to God, and no man can truly be obedient to God unless He does it by faith.

I'm sure Noah, the preacher of righteousness, was sure of the rain even though others weren't. Noah continued to build the ark, and others continued to party and drink even until he boarded the ark. Noah built it by faith. He followed the measurements he was given by faith. His family boarded with him by faith. And, righteousness was imputed unto him by faith. Noah was a man of faith. He was a man of God. But, most importantly, he was a man with God.

David was also a man who walked with God. Joseph walked with God. Paul walked with God. John walked with God. Luke walked with God. The list goes on, and on, and on. These men were men of God because they were men with God. They were not just men who spoke of God or believed in His existence. They were men who were fully-invested. Their cross was on their back, they were fully-clothed in their righteous armor, and their ways were sure. They stood valiantly for truth, and they were obedient.

Sir, I don't know what's been going on in your life, but I pray that you take a good look at it. Make a decision to be obedient to God. Like Thomas, you are hanging from the branch. Sin is crouching above you, and it is ready to eat away at you once it gets you in its grasp. It wants to devour you, just like the tiger wanted to devour Thomas. As you hang there, you also notice your past as it rears its head at you. It begins to eat away at what you're holding on to. It could be that you've trying to be faithful, but your past doesn't want you to forget the way you were. It wants to remind you of how you used to be. It wants to have you back. It wants to ruin you. Each bite it takes at you reminds you of how it wants to tear away at your present and, ultimately, end your future. But, even through all of this, you hear the assuring voice of God telling you to let go. He tells you that it will require courage and faith. You agree to it without ever really considering the consequences. All God wants you to do is let go. He wants you to let go of that branch you've been hanging on all your life. It's become a comfortable place for you, but, sooner or later, your arms are going to get tired. Sooner or later, the branch will break, and you will fall. You will have no other choice but to let go. You may think that this world will last forever. If you do, you're sadly mistaken. It will break just like that branch. Instead of waiting for it to break, just let go of it now. Let go of the pornography that has ruined your life for so many years. Let go of the fornication and sex that's eating away at your soul. Let go of the false religious games you've been playing. Let go of the religious rhetoric you've been using. Don't you want to know how it feels to truly live? If so, you, my brother, have to be willing to truly die! Let go of the pains of your past and refuse to go back to it.

Rise up with a greater level of readiness, and embrace the company of our God. Stop running from Him. Stop trying to hide from Him. Don't you know that He is everywhere and knows all? You cannot escape Him. You cannot go under Him, or go around Him, but you must get to Him through His Son, Jesus Christ.

Realize that we are in need of your talents. We are in need of your obedience to God. If you hear from God that it is time to begin a new thing or leave an old thing, then do it immediately. The entire trajectory of your life is changed in one decision to obey. If God is calling you to pioneer something using your gifts and talents, then you must. God has assigned people to you to be blessed by your obedience. Will you look beyond yourself in order to serve those around you? Realize that you are a man with God; thereby, you're becoming a man of God. Ultimately, your actions will prove the title.

THE MAN AND HIS PURPOSE

You are significant, important, superior in quality or character, of noble birth, powerful, influential, distinguished and first-rate. Your handprint is proof that you're different, peculiar, and set apart; it is God's stamp of approval that you are special. Don't allow for your circumstances to qualify you. Only allow God to qualify you. You are an ambassador who is called to be more than a conqueror. Don't settle for just anything.

What is your purpose? When you die, what do you want the world to remember you for? What will be the legacy you leave behind? I understand that this can be a very stressful thing to consider. You could be someone who isn't living life at all. Instead, you're allowing life to live you. You might be stuck in some dead-end job that only affords you the option to live from paycheck-to-paycheck. You could be the man who has found his purpose. You could be doing exactly what God has purposed and called you to do. No matter which man you are, you will have to make up your mind whether or not you will complete the assignment you've been given for your life. See, having an assignment is very important. We've all been given one by God. After discovering the assignment, we must be faithful to fulfill it whether we like it or not. It is no longer our will. Our assignment is all about God's will for us. Our goal is to just be obedient to what He has purposed for us.

Usually when we think about our purpose, we encounter some kind of fear. I know I feared what would happen if I submitted myself to God fully. I didn't want to become a preacher. I wanted to be a lawyer and a politician. The preacher and the lawyer essentially do the same thing, somewhat. Both of them are supposed to rightfully divide the truth. Unfortunately, the lawyer divides what's temporal, while the preacher divides what's eternal. Nonetheless, I need you to realize that the fear of the unknown is not needed. There is no reason for you to feel like you have to fear what God has for you. You must submit to it.

Honestly, submission to the assignment isn't the major problem most men face. The issue is actually discovering the assignment. We overcomplicate something that is very simple. If the assignment is from God, then we should seek Him for it. That means we seek Him in prayer until we hear His instructions. I've had many people to ask me how long should they stay in prayer. The answer is simple. You stay in prayer until you receive the answer you're after. You don't stop. You continue seeking God until you find Him. You continue knocking until He answers. You don't give up. You don't stop.

Be honest with yourself: What boundaries in your life are keeping you from being obedient? How long will you allow them to hinder you from doing all God has called you to do?

Men all around the world want to be successful. They see singers, rappers, athletes, entertainers, etc., and they begin to think that success must look like what they have. To the teen, success in nothing more than having straight-Ahing more than having straight-Aingers, rappers, athletes, entertainers, etc., and they begin That's not biblical success. Biblical success is defined as obedience. Noah was successful because he was obedient. Jonah, after his disobedience, was successful because he was obedient. Isaiah was successful because he was obedient. Jesus was successful because He was obedient. It doesn't matter how it looks to everyone else. Obedience is the mark of success for the believer. That may mean that you won't have the nice house or the nice cars. It doesn't matter in relation to eternity because, ultimately, it's all about being obedient to God. Ask yourself this question: What good is it for you to live a high-class life on earth, then die have spend eternity in hell? What good is it to work your whole life trying to get all the world's goods, but spend the rest of your eternity in hell? Consider eternity in relation to this life. Is all of your striving for these worldly things worth it? What good is it to stand before God and realize that all your working and striving was in vain? How would it feel to stand before God to hear Him say that you did a perfect job on the wrong assignment? What good is it, sir? What good is it? All my striving in the flesh has been worthless and useless. If it hasn't been born of God in prayer, then it's worthless. If it hasn't been born of God, then why even waste my time trying to pursue it? I'd advise you to let other worldly-minded men chase the things of this world. Instead, you chase God! Chase Him with everything in you. Turn your entire focus towards Him. Let everything you do be born of God. If it is, it will have passion and intensity. If it isn't born of God, it will be dead before it even gets started. It may have a lot of activity, but it will lack power. Only the things that are born of God will have the power that will cause change. That is what you want to do. That is what you want to pursue.

What are the areas of your life that are still not disciplined? Are you okay with living an undisciplined life? You may have it all together, but what about your fellow brothers? What about them? Who are you when no one else is looking? Are you just some undisciplined man? Are you the guy who tries to cut corners and make excuses? Are you the guy who allows for ignorance to lead him?

Read this carefully. You have a life to live, and you have an assignment to complete. At the end of your life, someone could write your biography. What would the title be? Would the entire book be about a man who made excuses, or would it be a book about a man who strived towards righteousness?

Finding your purpose isn't difficult, but it will take some labor. It will take some well-spent time being intimate with the Lord in prayer. It could take some much-needed fasting. It could require you to turn your television off so that you can finally sit and talk with the Lord. It will require something precious from you. What is that requirement? It's your life. Are you ready to give it? Count the cost, sir. Count the cost.

YOU ARE THE MAN

David is referred to as a man after God's own heart. He was a courageous military leader, a great king, and a slayer of Goliath, and a champion of the Philistines. It is evident that God was with David. He had such a passion and zeal for God. He also had an unshakeable hope in the kindness and mercy of the Lord. He was committed to God in all things, and his fear of the Lord was great, whether he was being considered last behind all his brothers or running from the tyrannical King Saul. He was a powerful military commander who was called to battle on many occasions. He was victorious as a conqueror, but, like most men, he could not conquer himself.

In contrast to all of his amazing qualities and accomplishments, he was not a perfect role model. Although a notable hero of faith, David was not without his failures. He was a liar, an adulterer, and a murderer. While the other kings were away at war, King David was walking along on his roof where he notices another man's wife, Bathsheba. He wants her. He sends for her. David is intimate with her, and he has her husband killed on the battlefield.

2 Samuel 12 reads, "Then the Lord sent Nathan to David. And he came to him and said, 'There were two men in one city, the one rich and the other poor. The rich man had a great many flocks and

herds. But the poor man had nothing except one little ewe lamb, which he bought and nourished; and it grew up together with him and his children. It would eat of his bread and drink of his cup and lie in his bosom, and was like a daughter to him. Now a traveler came to the rich man, and he was unwilling to take from his own flock or his own herd, to prepare for the wayfarer who had come to him; rather he took the poor man's ewe lamb and prepared it for the man who had come to him.'

Then David's anger burned greatly against the man, and he said to Nathan, 'As the Lord lives; surely the man who has done this deserves to die. 'He must make restitution for the lamb fourfold, because he did this thing and had no compassion.'

Now, I want you to read Nathan's response to David.

"Nathan then said to David, 'YOU ARE THE MAN!' Thus says the Lord God of Israel, 'It is I who anointed you king over Israel and it is I who delivered you from the land of Saul. I also gave you your master's house and your master's wives into your care, and I gave you the house of Israel and Judah; and if that had been too little, I would have added to you many more things like these! Why have you despised the word of the Lord by doing evil in His sight? You have struck down Uriah the Hittite with the sword, have taken his wife to be your wife, and have killed him with the sword of the sons of Ammon. Now therefore, the sword shall never depart from your house, because you have despised Me and have taken the wife of Uriah the Hittite to be your wife. Thus says the Lord, 'Behold, I will raise up evil against you from your own household; I will even take your wives before your eyes and give them to your companion, and he will lie with your wives in broad daylight. Indeed you did it secretly, but I will do this thing before all Israel, and under the sun.'

Then David said to Nathan, 'I have sinned against the Lord.' And Nathan said to David, 'The Lord also has taken away your sin; you shall not die. 'However, because by this deed you have given occasion to the enemies of the Lord to blaspheme, the child also that is born to you shall surely die.'"

It is difficult to imagine Nathan would need to rebuke the great and triumphant leader, King David. However, the message Nathan delivered was clear to David. David had to have his eyes opened to the truth. He had to realize one key truth—he is the man.

Brother, this book is for one purpose. It is for you to have your eyes opened to one truth. I want you to complete this book realizing one clear truth— Brother, YOU ARE THE MAN!

You are responsible for the poor, sinful decisions you make. You will be responsible for the family God places in your care. You will be responsible for the wife God will present to you to love all as Christ loves the Church. You are responsible for the children that you will be tasked to teach, train, and lead. The responsibility is not going to be passed any longer. Brother, YOU ARE THE MAN!

WORTHLESS SACRIFICE

I would like to imagine my sacrifice as something worthy enough to be praised, but it's not. I read about the martyrs before me, and I am so convicted. I look at my sacrifice and I count it as nothing. Think about the martyrs before us who gave their whole lives for Gospel spreading. Hebrews 11:35-38 says, "[They] were tortured and refused to be released, so that they might gain a better resurrection. Some faced jeers and flogging, while still others were chained an put in prison. They were stoned; they were sawed in two; they were put to death by the sword. They went about in sheepskins and goatskins, destitute, persecuted and mistreated-the world was not worthy of them. They wandered in deserts and mountains, and in caves and holes in the ground."

Wow! I look at my life, and it doesn't look anything like that. And, I'm not comparing or wishing that upon myself; however, I use this to greatly humble me. I must be humbled and brought to insignificance. I have yet to face jail time for preaching about Jesus. I have yet to be flogged, chained or jeered. My life is pretty easy. I've travelled from village to village preaching and telling others about Jesus, but I haven't faced that kind of persecution.

I remember being in Addis Ababa, Ethiopia in a home of one of the natives there. When I walked in, I noticed the pictures of Christ on the wall. I immediately knew that I was in a very safe place. I knew I wouldn't face any persecution in their home. I knew I was going to be well-protected and my words would be accepted. I'm not sure if you'll understand what I'll say next, but I must say it. Well, I didn't really want to go in the house. I felt bad for going in because I desired to go into the home of an unbeliever and potentially win another soul for Christ. Like Paul writes in Romans 10, I desire that my people are saved and they know Christ. To go into the home of a believer was a simple task. It wasn't difficult at all. The most of what I would have to war against would be unbelief in the person's heart. However, that was a small thing compared to anything else.

While in Addis Ababa, I preached at a church. It is a beautiful church filled with believers. The message of Christ has been captured in their hearts so much so that they now desire to go tell others about Christ. Every Saturday, they go into the streets and evangelize. The pastor, and my friend, goes into the city with them, sits among the forgotten and those who do not believe, and preach the Gospel to them. They literally give up their Saturdays to do it. Now, do I praise them for their sacrifice? No. Why? Well, this is not a sacrifice at all, this is what believers are told to do. It is the responsibility of the five-fold ministry gifts to build up the Body so they they can do the work of the Christ. And, there is no greater work than to spread the good news that Christ has died for our sins; yet, He rose from the dead on the third day, and now He lives. That is every believer's assignment. It isn't packaged in a ministry or given just to the committed. It is for every believer without exception. And, there doesn't have to be a time that you set aside to evangelize. In fact, every time you step outside the walls of yourself, you should be prepared to share Christ. And, if you find a believer, rejoice because they are few, and encourage him/her because she/he needs it. I may not praise them for their sacrifice, but I do applaud them for their obedience because they went into the uttermost parts and faced danger in the face for the sake of Christ. They faced rejection and potential death if they came upon someone who was so determined not to believe that he harmed them. I did not face such rejection while I stood behind the pulpit to teach to the people.

I remember thinking about how insignificant it was for me to stand in such a secure place and minister the Gospel. It was not dangerous by the least bit. Nonetheless, I preached with everything that was in me. I had to share all that Christ had so generously gave to me to the members of the church. I thought to myself, "Who am I to stand here and preach? I am younger than everyone who sits before me. I am less-educated. I am weaker. Yet, it is me who occupies the spot behind the podium." As I stood to speak, my knees began to buckle; my hands began to shake. I grew more and more nervous. I was many miles away from home. I felt as if I was unprepared and unqualified. As I stood there, the Lord said to me "Son, I am with you." That was all I needed. To have the Father of all creation to say He is with me was enough to cause every vibration in me to cease.

I preached, and I preached. Yet, I was still bothered. I desired so much for unbelievers to believe. Preaching in the safe church was an easy task. It's the least I can do as a disciple of Christ. It requires very little of me. Most importantly, it requires obedience. I understand that can be very difficult for many to do. So, I do not wish to make light of it at all.

For me, the desire to win souls was so strong that I forgot the importance of building up the members of the Body. I totally forgot how vital it was for me to go and minister to those who desire to learn so they may go and do the work.

I know this chapter may seem very foreign to many of you. In fact, some may say, "What is your point you're trying to make?" Honestly, I don't have one. For me, I strongly desire for men to be saved. I desire for men to grow and change. I desire for men to develop a loving relationship with God. I desire it so much. Yet, I cannot allow that desire to minimize the importance of teaching those who already believe so that they can do the work of the ministry.

To my pastoral friends, I pray that you desire to have souls changed for Christ. I pray that you desire men to leave the ways of the world and fall fully in love with Christ. That is my utmost prayer. At the same time, I pray that you desire to have the Word preached to you, and you preach it to others so we all may grow and change. That is my utmost desire and prayer. I understand your desire to develop and grow a big church, but consider the greater mission! Consider whether or not your desire is selfish and self-seeking. I can tell you that we greatly need more clergy in the field than we do in the pulpit. We need clergy who will stand outside the streets under the lampposts on the bench preaching the Gospel of Christ.

I ask that you consider your own life. Consider your own sacrifice. I pray you find your own sacrifice as nothing as I have mine. We can talk for hours about the safety of the church; however, I pray that you desire to cross that dotted line and step into a world of danger and improbability. You desire to be a man? Well, be dangerous! Consider your life as nothing, and choose to be obedient. Go where the Master commands. See and do as the Master commands of you. Don't seek to buy or prove His love. You don't have enough money or enough talent to do either. Just give of yourself the little you have left.

There are men and women who are laying down their lives. I have no right to do anything less. I'm convicted when I read about the martyrs before me. Men were beaten, tarred, feathered, set on fire, crucified upside down, jailed, and the list goes on. I heard reports of my brothers being shot in their stomachs because they would not denounce the Christ. I've read reports of men who were beaten and thrown in prison to be forgotten because they refused to deny Christ as Savior. These men ventured into the uttermost parts of the world where men would not set foot. They didn't go to the safety of the church. They didn't seek shelter with those who believed. They went right into the cities comprised of those who do not believe and spoke the Gospel truth. I know men who are living in countries where it is illegal to preach the Gospel; yet, they do it anyway. They boldly carry around their Bibles and tell strangers about Christ. They suffer persecution. They're threatened with death or prison; yet, they continue in faith. Their lives are foolish to unbelievers; yet, they are obedient to God anyway. Be strong, and fight the good fight of faith in honorable service to God!

I SURRENDER

I never wanted to be a preacher. I wanted to be a politician. Ironically, the preacher and the politician should have the same goals in mind; however, that is not always the case for both sides. Nonetheless, I wanted to be a statesman who stood for the people, elected by the people, and served along with the people; but God had other plans for me.

Throughout my high school and college career, I would rush to leadership roles, and I was oftentimes successful. My win-to-lose ratio was very impressive. I started my sophomore year in high school when I decided to seek the office of class president. At that time, I wasn't well-known or well-liked. I was not "popular," but I did know many of the "popular" people. I used those connections to my advantage. I campaigned as much as I possibly could to become the president of my sophomore class. I was climbing a very steep hill because I was campaigning against two women. Seeing that our class was made up of more women than men, I was already outmatched. However, I had a plan to counter it. We had to give speeches to our class so they would be able to make a well-informed decision on who they wanted to represent them for the school year. My two female opponents were ready to stand and deliver speeches that would bring me to my knees in humiliating defeat. However, I asked to go to the microphone first to do something that would prove advantageous for me. I asked both ladies to step forward, and I gave them flowers, thanked them for their campaigning, and I escorted them back to their seats. My plan to turn the women in the audience to my side had worked. Before giving my speech, I spoke with who we considered some of the "popular" kids in my class, and I asked them to stand up and clap during certain points of my speech. I had them to do this because I realized their ability to rouse emotions in their followers could be advantageous for me. I wanted the people who looked up to them to see their support for me. This, too, proved to be very advantageous for me. After the speeches, after the dust settled, and at the end of the day, they got ready to announce the winner. I had been elected class president.

That was a big deal for me. Just one year before that election, I was the fat kid who always wore a big bubble jacket everywhere I went because I was self-conscious about my body. It would be 99 degrees outside, but I would still have on that jacket. I would be drenched, but I wouldn't take the jacket off. I sat in the back of the lunchroom, and I ate alone. I felt ashamed that I was always hungry. To add injury to insult, I had a senior to come and steal some cookies I just purchased for myself. He took them from right in front of me. When I got up to chase him through the cafeteria, all the students started to laugh at me. At that moment, all the pain I felt from the bullying I received from my past began to rise back inside of me. I ran out of the cafeteria to a classroom and I began to cry. When I got home that day, I sat in my room and I began to write the most hateful poems I had ever written in my entire life. It was at that point that I wanted to see people dead, and I wanted to know they suffered before their death. Knowing this, I pray it helps you to understand the importance of standing before those same students and being elected their president.

I didn't stop there, though. I went on to become president of many other extracurricular organizations including, but not limited to, the Future Farmers of America, Future Business Leaders of America, Key Club, etc. The year I was elected president did something to me inside that was both beneficial and damning. Yes, I was confident, but my confidence was in myself.

I went on to be elected president of my class my junior and senior year as well. My junior year was a busy one. I was elected president of seven different extracurricular clubs at school, vice president of two, and treasurer of one. I was a busy man. I was also chosen and qualified myself for the Governor's Honors Program, a six-week program where students are chosen and tested to go to a college-style summer program with other gifted students in Georgia. While at Valdosta State University for 6-weeks, I majored in Social Studies with a minor in Counseling. I really needed that class because God knows I had some major issues. Nonetheless, the class was about as helpful as a no-legged man in a butt-kicking contest. I also began to win speaking awards through different county and state competitions. My confidence was beginning to soar through the roof, but it was destroying me.

I was your regular over-achiever who won all the awards and held all the leadership titles. I wasn't served my first defeat until I ran for president of the Future Business Leaders of America on the state level. I gave a speech to over 40,000 high school students and advisors on why I should be elected their president. It came down between Becky Garrett and me. I'll never forget that moment when they called out the winner of the contest to be Becky Garrett. That was my first loss, and I took it rather hard. I soon rebounded by starting a mentoring organization at my old high school, in which, I called it "Gentlemen of Quality" or "GQ."

By the end of my high school career, I was really into myself. The awards and acclaim got to my head, and my pride was through the roof. I was mean as a rattlesnake, ready to strike at any victim that came close to me. I was hard-hearted, and I was a manipulator. I would sit and read books about war and deception to learn ways of how to deceive people to get what I wanted. I began to study dictators like Stalin, Hitler, etc. to understand their thought process. I wanted to rule the world, and I wanted to kill Christians. Why Christians? I couldn't understand why someone whom Christians believed in would allow me to be ridiculed in the days of my youth. I couldn't understand why someone that they loved would allow them to continue to live like heathens. It was crazy to me, and I hated to be around them. In actuality, they weren't my problem. I was my own problem, and pride was taking me to my downfall.

I applied to 3 different colleges: Morehouse College in Atlanta, Georgia, George Washington University in Washington D.C., and the University of Georgia in Athens, Georgia. I was accepted into all of them, but I chose to go to University of Georgia. I had my reasons. They weren't good reasons, but they were reasons nonetheless. Once I got on the University of Georgia campus, I began to scout out the competition. I soon became president of my community hall that was made up of about 1,100 freshmen. Then, I ran for a senator position for the Franklin College of Arts and Design with the Vote Naked Party. Most of the Party was defeated, but I was elected senator of my college. That was big deal for me. I was also chosen for the Freshmen Board for Student Government Association. I was making a name for myself pretty quickly on campus, and I had my eyes on the presidency of SGA. I wouldn't get a chance to go for it though.

While walking along a path back to my dormroom, I saw a piece of paper on the ground that mentioned a Bible. I decided to call the number just so I could argue the irrelevance of God with them. The two guys agreed to come to my dormroom to talk to me. One afternoon, I heard a knock on my door. I opened it to two men with short-sleeved white shirts, black pants, and a nametag on. Yes, I was preparing to sit with Mormons. After talking with them, I decided to go to the service that Sunday. I didn't have a clue what they were talking about, but I did know I *loved* the fact that the service was only 30 minutes long. They also gave free pizza to those who came. I was still a bit uneasy about the whole thing, but I was assured that I would become a Mormon after a conversation with some elders. They said the Mormon Church was looking for young, ethnic, charismatic leaders to bring more into the fold. In my prideful eyes, that was my chance to have a position that could eradicate Christianity forever. Yes, I was crazy.

Soon, I was asked to go on a mission's trip to Indonesia, but I refused to go because of the standards. They said I wouldn't have a car, I'd have to wear a set ensemble, and my schedule was already made out for me. Sorry, but that wasn't going to happen for me. A couple months later, I decided to go to a charismatic church service by a very charismatic preacher. At the end of his sermon, he began to talk about Jesus. I was compelled to know more about Him from that moment. I would drive almost 2 hours every Sunday and Wednesday night to attend the service hoping to hear more about Jesus. Soon, my relationship with God was beginning to blossom, and my desire to want more of Him increased. About a year after successful campaigns at the University of Georgia and growing in my relationship with the Father, I left college, moved back in with my parents, and I sat and waited on God to speak to me concerning what He wanted me to do with my life. I had a teacher to ask me, "What is your contingency plan for failure?" I told her, "I don't have a contingency plan for failure because I'm not planning to fail."

First, I began working at a restaurant as a server. It was a humbling experience. I went from being the guy who was voted most likely to succeed to the guy who was serving food and waiting tables. I soon quit the job because my girlfriend-at-the-time had an emergency. Her father was dying quickly due to many forms of cancer. He was in Florida, and we were in Georgia. I couldn't allow her, her mom, and her sister to drive all the way down there by themselves. That trip turned out to be the last time I would see him alive, so it was well-worth it. But, I was back to not having a job or an idea of what

God wanted me to do. A couple months after quitting my job, I got a call from the pastor of the charismatic church telling me that God told him I was supposed to work for him. Considering the fact that I never wanted to work at a church, I was a little apprehensive. Nonetheless, I did it anyway. That entire journey lasted for almost 4 years. In the midst of that journey, I was still focused on my political aspirations. I decided to run for a state representative seat in Georgia. I was well on my way to a successful campaign, but I had to drop it because of residency issues. Then, I decided to run for a councilman seat in the city I lived, Jonesboro. I thought I would have this one in the bag. Unfortunately, the city district lines didn't extend to my home. I left the meeting distraught and confused as to why I could never seem to secure a political or governmental position. I went home and I called Heather, who I was courting at the time. I told her how upset and confused I was about the whole thing. I got off the phone with her, and I got right in the bed with my full suit still on. I lay down on my pillow, and God began to speak to me. He said, "If you won't do what I've called you to do, then why should I open your eyes in the morning?" I opened by eyes, jumped out of the bed, got on my knees, and I told God, "I surrender. Okay, I'll do it." That was the beginning of my ministerial life as a preacher. It was a moment that revolutionized and changed my life.

After years of aspiring to reach my political goals, I decided to put them aside to accept the mission God had prepared for me. Little did I realize, He had a lot of crap to get out of me.

It didn't matter though, because I surrendered. I surrendered my life, my plans, my actions, my duties, my responsibilities to Him.

THE ULTIMATE SACRIFICE

A treasure worth finding is a treasure worth keeping. A treasure worth inheriting is a treasure worth maintaining. What treasure in this world is worth finding and worth inheriting? There are two treasures that come to mind. For every man, the first is the kingdom of heaven, and the second is his family. Matthew 13:44-46 reads, "The kingdom of heaven is like a treasure hidden in the field, which a man found and hid again; and from joy over it he goes and sells all that he has and buys that field."

There is a treasure in a field, and a man searches and finds that treasure. After finding this treasure, it is evident that he realizes that there is no greater treasure worth searching for or obtaining. There is nothing else that can compare to the treasure he finds in the field, and there is nothing that can substitute that treasure. It is priceless, significant, and unable to be left behind. Then, the Scriptures state that he goes and sells all that he has to purchase that field. Notice that he did not sell all of his belongings to purchase the treasure. He wanted the entire field! This shows the significance, relevance, and power of the treasure. It is so significant that it brings significance to everything that surrounds it—no matter how insignificant it may seem to others. Understand that the significance is not the field. The significance is the treasure.

The man is not pleased with just finding the treasure. The verse reads that he hides the treasure again. Then, it says that his joy leads him to sell all he has to purchase the entire field. It did not say he sold only those things he did not want anymore. It did not say he took his highest offering to the altar to provide a sacrifice for the treasure. It did not say he gave a percentage of what he earned. It said he gave all he had. Think about it for a moment. Think about everything that you have to your name. That could include your awards, your accolades, your clothes, your food, and your books. It is anything that has a price, and it does not matter how high the price may be. Then, consider finding a treasure hidden in a field. The treasure is worth so much to you that you go and sell it all. You do not leave anything behind. You take it all with you to sell. Then, you take that money to buy the entire field. The price of the field is not what is important because it is evident that it is extremely costly. Your joy overflows into an action of ultimate sacrifice. You have nowhere else to turn or go except back to that treasure and that field. If you wants to build again, it will be on that field and not on anything else.

Why is this significant, and what does it have to do with you? I want you to focus on the sacrifice: the focus of the sacrifice, and the meaning behind the sacrifice. When we sacrifice, we give up something that is costly to us in order to gain something of greater significance. We consider the loss we are going to incur, but we realize the gain of the sacrifice is greater than the value of the loss. To sacrifice is to dispose of whatever we have regardless of the value of it. We realize that it is a sacrifice and, in this situation, we realize just how costly the sacrifice is; however, the man still makes it.

Now, I want you to consider the field. Consider the property where the treasure rests. We have read that the man sold all he had, so it is just fine to assume he had nothing else besides that treasure and that field. Since the man had nothing else, we must ask where the man will live. Where will he spend his time? Where will he begin to start a new life? The answer is clear—he will begin again on that field.

Luke 14:28-33 reads, "For which one of you, when he wants to build a tower, does not first sit down and calculate the cost to see if he has enough to complete it? Otherwise, when he has laid a foundation and is not able to finish, all who observe it begin to ridicule him, saying, 'This man began to build and was not able to finish.' Or what king, when he sets out to meet another king in battle, will not first sit down and consider whether he is strong enough with ten thousand men to encounter the one coming against him with twenty thousand? Or else, while the other is still far away, he sends a delegation and asks for terms of peace. So then, none of you can be My disciple who does not give up all his own possessions."

That is a powerful set of verses that I recommend you meditate on day and night. Jesus says these powerful words even though they were penned by Luke. Jesus explains the sacrifice of service in such a way that it cannot be misunderstood. I have heard preachers use these verses to imply that men should not act or build. However, notice that Jesus did not say not to build. He stressed the importance of considering the cost of building before setting out to build. I am sure the man who found the treasure realized just how costly it would be to attain it. However, the cost did not matter. He was willing to give up everything he had to obtain it. He had to consider the cost of the treasure and the entire field. Then, he realized that obtaining it was so costly that he had to sell everything he had just to obtain it. That is some sacrifice right there. Now that he is left with nothing but a treasure in a field, he is able to do something that men seldom do today—he is able to consider building on that field. It does not matter how much he has given up to obtain the field because he is willing to give up everything to purchase it. He is left with no other possessions, and he is on his way to giving the ultimate sacrifice.

Now, why is this significant to you? What does this have to do with you and your possessions? Brother, this has everything to do with your sacrifice. Are you willing to give up your life for such a costly treasure as the kingdom of heaven? I want to take this a step further. Sir, are you willing to give up your life for your future spouse and your children? Are you willing to sell everything you have just to have the riches that are located in the treasure you have hidden in the field? I am not asking if you are willing to lay it aside. If you lay it aside, there is a possibility that you will try to go and pick it back up. I am asking if you are willing to get rid of it altogether. Are you willing to sacrifice not only your possessions but also your life? Are you willing to die for the kingdom of heaven's sake? Have you sat down to consider the cost of what you are either saying you want to build or are currently building?

You could be someone who desires to be married and begin a beautiful family someday. Let me ask you a serious question: Have you considered the cost? Are you prepared to sacrifice your life for that woman and for those children? Are you willing to give up the selfish ways of your single life to cling tightly your bride and your children? Do you seriously understand the responsibility that has been given to you as it relates to your future wife and your children?

The man who sets out to build without considering the cost will be ridiculed because he was unable to finish it due to his ignorance. Consider how many marriages are ruined today because men haphazardly and ignorantly enter into a covenant that they do not consider the cost of. This may pierce your heart, but I need to get in that heart of yours so you may not only read, but also understand and feel what I am saying to you. Are you that man? Are you that man who failed to consider the cost? Are you the man who went out in the field, say the treasure, greatly desired it, but decided against it because you felt as if what you had was more valuable than the treasure you found in the field? Are you that man? Understand that you are not answering these questions for me. You're answering these questions for you, and your future wife and children depend on it. Your life depends on it. Your eternity depends on it.

Have you given the ultimate sacrifice? Have you taken all you have to the merchant to sell, just so you can have the treasure you hid in the field? Have you considered your family at home or the family you want to build? Have you considered the sacrifice? Have you considered the heart that is needed for such a sacrifice? And, are you willing to be that sacrifice?

Sir, I do not care how much money you have in the bank. I do not care your title or your position. I do not care about your car or the home you reside in. I do not care about what logo is on your clothing to give the appearance of riches to others. I do not care how often you vacation. I do not care about the size of your penis or the number of women you have abused in the name of lust. However, I do care about your heart. I want to know where it lies. Does it lie with the prostitutes in the street, with your boys every Friday night, on the golfing range, at your job, in the strip club, etc.? Or, does it lie firmly in the hands of God? Are you willing to turn that heart of yours over to God and reconcile with Him through our Savior, Jesus Christ? If you are not, then I pray God has mercy on your soul. There should be no way you can read these words and still consider your old way of living and your current possessions as more valuable than your God and your family.

Will you consider this, man? Will you consider your eternity and your God? The momentary pleasure of today or the value you have placed on these earthly things will perish. Stay focused on the things of eternity instead of being focused on the temporary things of today. Stay firm in the Lord, and He will lead and guide you into all truth. Yes, brother, this is for you. This is about your life. This is about your relationship with God. This is about your ultimate sacrifice.

I remember the first time I ever heard the true Gospel preached. I could not help but to weep. I had never heard such passion and conviction from a preacher before in my entire life. Then, I heard a message from David Wilkerson entitled "A Call to Anguish." My wife was in Michigan on business, and I was all alone that night. I listened to that message, and I immediately began to weep. I cried for hours uncontrollably. Each time I would listen to these messages being preached, I would weep because I was realizing the cost associated with such a great treasure. When I sat down to study my biblical responsibility as a husband, I began to weep because I understood what I did not understand before I got married. When I sat down to learn about my responsibility as a father, I began to weep because I realized the cost involved. I listened to a sermon by Paul Washer entitled "The Cost of Not Following Jesus," and I wept aloud because I realized the cost for those who choose the possessions instead of the treasure. I realized how much I needed the treasure. I realized how the cost associated with obtaining and finding such a treasure. And, I realized that I would have to give the ultimate sacrifice to retain that treasure. That ultimate sacrifice was my life. I sat down at my desk one day to study, and the Lord began to deal with my heart. I knew I had not given my entire life to Him. My tears were tears of sorrow because I knew my ignorance was leading me to destruction. And, if the man, who is tasked to lead his family, is led by ignorance to destruction, then where do you think his family is headed? Yes, they are all headed to destruction. I realized the responsibility that was placed on my shoulders, and I asked God, "Why all this responsibility? It is too hard!" But, I realized that this life is not meant to be comfortable. We, as men, are called to war by equipping ourselves with the whole armor of God. We are called to pray without ceasing, and give our strict attention to studying God's Word. We are called to turn away from this world, and be transformed by the renewing of our mind. There is no comfort in sacrifice. That is why it is called sacrifice. It is supposed to mean something. It is supposed to be valuable. It is supposed to be costly. It is supposed to be meaningful.

Have you considered the cost of your sacrifice? And, are you willing to give the ultimate sacrifice of your life for your Lord, your future wife and family?

Understand that repentance means turning and going in a new direction. That means you no longer go in the same way you were once going. This means you will have to learn and become knowledgeable on the things you did not know. This means you will have to keep your oath you made to your family as you sat before them repenting. This means you have to forsake those things of the past so that you may walk confidently and righteously into the future. This is the ultimate sacrifice, and, yes, it is your life. Sacrifice it.

IN CONCLUSION

As we get towards the end of this book, I want to pour into you some things that have really helped me on my journey. I'm not putting them in any particular order. Just take from them what you will, and be sure to apply them to your life where you see fit.

Don't run from your problems; instead, run from sin. Sin is deadly, and it will do everything in its power to keep you prisoner.

Don't resist righteousness; instead, resist temptation. Sin will knock on the door of your heart. Do not answer it. Continue to set your mind on what's holy and excellent. Begin to pray or sing to God aloud. I've found it to be very difficult to sing Amazing Grace and watch pornography at the same time unless my heart was cold as ice and hard as a rock.

Don't bury your purpose; instead, bury your past. Leave what happened behind you, and begin to focus on the present. The goal is not for you to revert back to who you used to be. Instead, begin to move forward in your life.

Stand up for truth, or risk falling for foolishness.

Make God's standard of holiness your standard, and don't deviate from it. Never forget that we are to love God and love others as we love ourselves. That simple truth sums up the Ten Commandments. In total, loving God represents the first four Commandments. Loving others sums up the last six. Teach them to your children, and make sure you portray an excellent example to them by following them yourself.

Do away with pornographic material in your life. Get rid of it. Throw it away for once, and do away with it forever.

Show respect to your elders, even those who you don't think deserve it. Saying "yes, sir" and "yes, ma'am" wasn't just a Southern thing. It was something we learned to do out of respect for our elders. When an elder walks along the sidewalk, you step off to allow them to continue walking on the sidewalk. When you notice an elder standing up, be the first one to give up your seat so she or he can sit down. Be sure to check on the elders in your community. See if they need their grass cut, their tree limbs cut down, some extra food, or a listening ear.

Walk with confidence, not arrogance. When sitting, don't slump in the chair. When standing, don't slouch down. When talking, be clear and concise. Think before you speak, and be humble enough to ask for advice from others. Look others in the eyes when you talk to them. Make sure your handshake is firm, but don't make it too firm. Make sure you brush your teeth and floss regularly. It's also a wise idea to wash your tongue. Oftentimes, a lot of food and waste rests on your tongue even after brushing your teeth.

Worrying is useless. Worrying says, "I don't truly believe, so my only option is to take charge and do it my way." Refuse to worry about anything. Instead, have faith in God. He will see you through. I'd be a fool to say I truly believe, yet continue to worry. I may as well say that I don't truly believe, but I just want to pretend like I do.

Drama kings and queens desire a stage to perform; don't give them one. They love to play the blame game. It's always everyone else's fault. They never consider their own part to play. Don't give them the indication that you are willing to sit down to watch their performance. If you give them some attention, they will definitely perform.

Don't try to schedule God around your daily activities. Instead, schedule your daily activities around God. Set time to pray and study the Word of God. Don't put it off. Make it a priority.

Don't be afraid to be different. You're unique, and that is okay. Don't be afraid to go against what's popular, especially when what's popular isn't holy. Don't be afraid to say what needs to be said even when others around you are silent. Don't be afraid to rise up to the occasion to be the man God has called you to be. Just don't fear.

Be sure to tip those who serve you, and tip them generously. In some cultures, it is customary to tip someone before they begin the task. Nowadays, we like to wait to see what they do and base their tip on their performance. Either way, be generous when you tip your server, your tailor, your barber, your shoe shiner, your housekeepers, etc.

Be sure to keep your shoes shined. Search around for a good shoe shiner who puts care into seeing your shoes sparkle as if they were brand new. Instead of purchasing a cheap pair of shoes, invest in a nice pair. Then, continue to get them shined. Also, ask the shoe shiner to put brakes on the bottom of your shoes. They will allow for your soles to last longer.

Learn how to tie a tie knot correctly. There are many different methods. Find the one that works best for you, and stick with it.

Be sure to say "please," "thank you," and "forgive me." Never forget that you are a humble man, and humble men are not too prideful to offer humble compliments.

Before going in public, be sure to check your zipper, clean your ears, check for any debris in the crevices of your eyes, remove any debris from in and around your nose, and be sure to make sure nothing is stuck between your teeth or around your mouth. It's also wise to do a breath test. If the smell is questionable, or if someone mentions it to you, go and do something about it.

When answering the phone and someone asks to speak to you, say, "This is he" instead of "This is him."

When someone asks you how you're feeling or doing, respond by saying, "I'm well," not "I'm good." Food is good, but people are well. Things can taste or smell good. The word "well" has to do with health and wellness. They're asking you how you feel, not how you taste.

Be considerate of others around you. Pay attention to what you're doing, and make sure you're aware of how it affects others.

Make sure you arrive to an appointment early. Don't show up late. Being late is unacceptable. If there's a problem that will prevent you from being on time, be sure to communicate it to those who are waiting on you. Another person's time is too valuable to waste; therefore, don't waste it by being late.

For more wisdom tips, I want to encourage you to read the Book of Proverbs. I'm sure it will help you as much as it helped me along my journey. I want to also encourage you to take all you've read and apply it to your life. Become accountable. Confront your fears and your struggles. Truly encounter Christ, and be transformed. This is not a game. With all that being said, I must ask you one question: So, you want to be a man?

Made in the USA
Columbia, SC
23 July 2017